Wild Tracks

Wild Tracks
Trevor Fishlock

seren

seren is the book imprint of
Poetry Wales Press Ltd
Wyndham Street, Bridgend, CF31 1EF
Wales

Book based on the HTV Wales series 'Fishlock's Wild Tracks'
produced by Ffilmiau'r Nant.

Published with the kind permission of HTV Wales Limited

ISBN 1-85411-225-2

Seren works with the financial support of the
Arts Council of Wales

Printed in Plantin by The Cromwell Press, Trowbridge

Contents

Introduction

I have been fortunate, as a foreign correspondent, to have travelled in more than sixty countries, to have marvelled at many of the world's great natural spectacles. But, as if drawn by some agreeable magnetic force, I am always pulled back to Wales. The crossing of the border never fails to trigger in me a feeling of excitement and expectation. It's partly history and roots, I suppose. My paternal grandfather was one of those English wetbacks who crossed the Severn to join the coal rush in the Rhondda at the end of the last century. He married a Welsh girl. My father was born in Pontypridd, quitting Wales, as so many did, during the depression.

I never tire of the look of Wales. Much of the joy of exploring this country lies in its astonishing variety. It is a jigsaw of landscapes. Turn the corner, crest a ridge, and in front of you is spread another completely different panorama or charming vignette, a delicate watercolour or a robust oil. In its craggy carapace, the country looks a fortress; and when big-shouldered clouds gather in strength over the mountains, it can appear forbidding as well as grand. But it is also a land of inviting, half-open doors, just waiting to be pushed.

The landscape, though, is only half the story. The rest lies in the people. It may be fanciful, but it seems to me that there's a certain spirit of human endurance, of determined persistence, which matches the hard and ancient rock. And then there are the voices of a story-telling people, recalling and embellishing incidents and comedies, revealing the treasures in the accretions of history.

The stories seem to grow on trees. There is barely a house, a hill, a churchyard, gully, beach or chapel that does not have a tale attached to it. I like the fables and the legends as well as the documented history. They are part of the fabric. And I live in hope of meeting one of the shy mermaids who live along the curling coasts.

When I went to Wales as staff correspondent of *The Times* of London at the end of the 1960s I was lucky in my tutors. One of them was Wynford Vaughan-Thomas, whose gifts as a raconteur had deep foundations in his scholarship. His encyclopaedic knowledge of Wales matched his exuberant love for it; and he used to say that Wales is a country of just the right size for one person to get to know well in one lifetime.

Once, when I was planning a walk across Wales, from south to north, I went to Wynford for advice. He took my map and marked out a route for me. My planned one-hour lunchtime interview turned into a history lesson, punctuated by laughter, anecdotes and scandalous stories, that lasted all afternoon and into the evening. I made that journey – nine days from the Rhondda to Caernarfon, including half a day on horseback – and since then I have made many more expeditions, some of them gentle, some of them rather more rugged.

Since I love walking, history, humour and writing about Wales, you can imagine how delighted I am to be involved in *Fishlock's Wild Tracks* for HTV, my passport to many happy days. The programmes mine a rich vein. In every patch of Wales people love their land – and the land has a lot to say for itself. It is teamwork, of course, this mixture of words and pictures; and the keystone is Wil Aaron, who made his name as a television director during many assignments abroad before he returned to his Welsh roots. He matches his film-making brilliance to a passion for history and his homeland.

The framework of the walks is that, in general, they can be completed in one day by a person of average fitness. Some are not especially demanding, but, since this is Wales, I've done my share of panting to the top of steep climbs. I make a point of starting each walk with a good breakfast and try to ensure that the rigours of a day in the open are rewarded by an excellent dinner. With this goal in mind, I have found some lovely restaurants and hotels.

We keep to the footpaths shown on the Ordnance Survey Pathfinder and Landranger series of maps and I will admit that we have been lost once or twice. In some parts, footpaths are hard to find or are so overgrown that they are almost impassable. In my experience, farmers are usually helpful in setting you on the right track. Most of them are interested in the history of their neighbourhoods and often have very good tales to tell. The vital elements of the programme are the ever-surprising land and people, Wales speaking eloquently and entertainingly for itself.

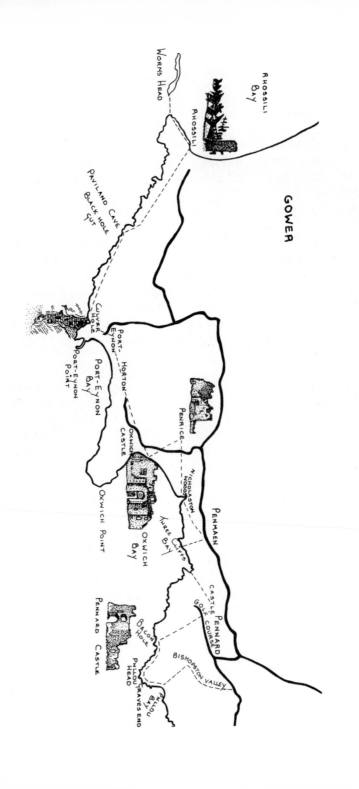

GOWER

WORMS HEAD

RHOSSILI BAY

RHOSSILI

PAVILAND CAVE

BLACK HOLE GUT

CULVER HOLE

PORT-EYNON POINT

PORT-EYNON BAY

PORT-EYNON

HORTON

OXWICH CASTLE

PENRICE

NICHOLASTON WOODS

OXWICH POINT

OXWICH BAY

THREE CLIFFS

PENMAEN

PENNARD GOLF COURSE

CASTLE

PENNARD CASTLE

BACON HOLE

PWLLDU HEAD

BISHOPSTON VALLEY

PWLLDU BAY

GRAVES END

1. GOWER

Where the deer and rhinoceros roamed

I was up early for a proper Gower breakfast: rashers of bacon with a large spoonful of glutinous and glistening laverbread. I like to fancy that this delicious indigo seaweed does for me what spinach does for Popeye.

The sunny dawn promised a fine day and the radio forecast was optimistic, too. I couldn't wait to get going. Gower is an exciting promontory of caves and I looked forward to exploring a number of them as I worked my way around the peninsula from Bishopston to the rocky sphinx of Worm's Head.

Wynford Vaughan-Thomas, who roamed Gower as a boy during his holidays before the First World War, used to say that Gower was a secret that people in Swansea hugged to themselves. It gave him pleasure all his life to know that just around the headland lay Gower's glory.

I marched easily for two miles through the dappled glades of the Bishopston Valley and paused to watch a woodpecker hard at work on a tree. He sounded like a shipyard riveter. The path emerged where the sparkling stream has its rendezvous with the sea at Pwlldu, the Black Pool. The bulky shoulder of Pwlldu Head rises three hundred feet and below it lies a pebble beach that makes a noise like broken crockery beneath your feet.

Nearby is a remnant of a quarrying village that once had a famous thirst, although the two remaining pubs are now private houses. In the last century limestone was blasted out of the cliff and loaded onto sledges which clattered in gullies down the slopes to ships waiting in the little bay. These gullies remain and an iron mooring ring is still fastened to a rock. The ships were known as muffies and ferried the limestone to kilns on the Devon coast where it was burnt for fertilizer. The men and women who sweated out their days in this quarry found evening solace in the pubs. Their labour was always exhausting, frequently crippling and sometimes fatal.

Heather Holt, who lives in one of the former pubs, walked with me up the narrow path to Graves End, a desolate, wind-blasted spot above the cliff, and showed me a stone circle half-concealed in the bracken. It marks the grave of up to ninety men drowned when the ship *Caesar* was driven ashore in 1760.

Many of these unfortunates had been manacled under the hatches, having been rounded up in Swansea by a Royal Navy press gang. Heather told me the chilling story handed down in her family – that the ship's captain and the mate had crawled over the bowsprit to the safety of the rocks as the *Caesar* was pounded to pieces. Their ears were filled with the screams of the doomed chained men in the hold.

The path is steep in parts but spectacular views repay the climb. I found the memorial stone on the cliff at Pennard which marks the place where Vernon Watkins loved to sit and stare at the sea and frame his verses. There's a fragment of one of them on the memorial:

> I have been taught the script of the stones
> And I know the tongue of the waves.

Watkins met Dylan Thomas in Pennard and the two poets formed a lifelong friendship. They were chalk and cheese in a way: Thomas rumbustious and Watkins a modest clerk in Lloyds Bank most of his days.

Hunts Bay: sculpted by Ice Age glaciers

Nineteenth-century explorers digging in the Gower caves found the bones of mammoths, rhinoceroses, elephants, bears and lions. These finds astonished scholars and revolutionised thinking about the prehistoric period. No-one had imagined that such marvellous creatures had lived in Britain. Gradually it became clear that before the sea swept in thousands of years ago the Bristol Channel was a vast plain, like the Serengeti of Africa, with immense wandering herds of game.

I descended the rough and steep corkscrew track to the cave called Bacon Hole. In the years when the press gangs roamed, local sailors and fishermen found refuge in secret places such as this. I could imagine how pleased the men must have been when their wives and mothers came down the path with food.

In 1912 Bacon Hole was the focus of excitement. On a wall deep inside the cave, explorers found ten horizontal red stripes. At once these were taken for prehistoric cave paintings, like those found in France, and an expert was summoned from France to examine them. He nodded and said it was possible they had been daubed by early artists. A heavy iron grille was erected to protect

Three Cliffs Bay: a Gower showpiece

the walls from sightseers. But it was later determined that the mysterious stripes were 'painted' by iron oxide oozing through the rocks. They were the colour of breakfast rashers, hence Bacon Hole. The stripes and a rusty section of the iron grille are still there.

My calf muscles felt the strain as I toiled up the cliff. But once on the top I had the comfort of walking a long stretch of springy turf over the golf course to Pennard Castle. Although the castle's situation is romantic it has little to say for itself, its history being pretty thin. It was built in the thirteenth century and was reduced to a husk by the sixteenth. The ruin is said to be the home of a ghost, a winged hag with sunken eyes; and perhaps the golfers blame her for their bad shots.

Nearby lie the ruins of a church, buried by sand. This happened to other buildings in south Wales and it can be imagined that the castle, too, was overwhelmed by mountains of sand moved by the force of great gales. On several occasions, shifting sands changed the appearance of the landscape.

I slithered down the meandering path into the grand arena of Three Cliffs Bay, one of the loveliest spectacles in Wales with its yellow sands and pyramid cliffs. But beware: there are treacherous

The slithery path to Three Cliffs Bay

currents not far offshore.

Using the stepping stones to cross the stream, I glanced up to see the castle at its most dramatically photogenic, silhouetted on the edge of the cliff, waiting to star in a King Arthur epic.

I made for Penmaen Burrows, another place where drifting sands buried a medieval church, and climbed to a rock balcony high on the Great Tor. The view was another wonder, the dazzling sands of Oxwich Bay stretching away to the far distance. In this crystal moment of the morning, I felt I had the whole of Gower to myself, as alone as Robinson Crusoe; then I spied a distant dot, a Friday figure, a Girl Friday as it happened, the sands spread like a golden cloak for her to walk upon.

In a short while I was out of the sunshine and walking through the lush and shady Nicholaston Woods, as if I had stepped under a parasol. Many of the plants here are rare and exotic; and there is no other place like it in Wales.

The path winds its way below the limestone edge to Penrice. The first castle was built here by a Norman conqueror. For three hundred and fifty years the land was held by the Mansels, who backed the right horses of history, married shrewdly and became mighty landowners when Henry VIII broke up the monasteries and

Penrice Castle: one of Gower's great houses

put half the land of England and Wales up for grabs.

Later, the Mansel Talbots built the classic corn-coloured Penrice mansion and developed the land around it as a sublime park. Judith Methuen-Campbell told me that when her husband inherited the magnificent house from his grandmother he demolished forty-three rooms simply to make the place manageable. There's a strong sense of continuity, she reflected, and 'when a place like this has been in your family this long you don't want to be the one who breaks the chain.'

William Henry Fox Talbot, the pioneer of photography, spent much of his youth at Penrice. He seemed to those around him to be a magician. By imprisoning light in a box, capturing an instant of life, he changed for ever our way of remembering. He revealed the mysteries of the camera to his cousins who became, in turn, trailblazers of photography in Wales.

Oyez, oyez: the Crying Stone, Penrice

In Penrice village I inspected two fascinating monuments, the Crying Stone and the Murder Stone. On the Crying Stone the town crier planted his feet to bellow his announcements and parish news. The Murder Stone, in the churchyard, has a grim history. It records the name of 'Mary, wife of James Kavanagh of Penmaen, who was murdered by ... ' and there is a blank space for the name of the unknown murderer; as if to say that the Almighty knows who it is and that there will be retribution in another place.

The path brought me to Oxwich where the Mansels built a castle. To this they added a large pigeon house to ensure that there was an alternative food supply in times when winter meat was scarce. Glenys Fuge, the curator, told me the story of the gold brooch that was found in the grounds in 1968. 'A workman took away a barrowload of rubble and while he was disposing of it some chickens pecked at the freshly-uncovered soil. When the man returned the brooch was glinting in the earth.' It is now in the National Museum of Wales.

It turned out to be part of the treasure of King Edward II, a weak and wretched man, nothing at all like his father Edward I, the conqueror of Wales. The brooch was lost around 1325 when Edward II was on the run from Isabella, his ruthlessly ambitious and scheming queen, known to her enemies as the 'She-Wolf'. Edward was captured in Wales and horribly murdered by his wife's thugs.

Looking over a hedge in Horton I saw a strange, dream-like spectacle, a garden full of heads looking for legs – and legs in

A crop of heads in Peter Nicholas's garden

17

search of heads, like some fantastic dating agency. At the back of the house I found Peter Nicholas, a genial fellow, working with his chisel on a slab of Portuguese marble. In the stone his artist's eye could see the form of a sea goddess. He was, painstakingly, bringing her to life.

'Most people plant flowers in their gardens,' Peter said, 'but I plant my sculptures. Men have worked the stone around here for hundreds of years, so that, as a sculptor, I feel happily part of local traditions.'

In the last century, pretty Port-Eynon earned its living by oyster fishing and quarrying. Horses hauled its lifeboat into the sea and John Beynon recited to me his verses on the true story of the lifeboat horse. One afternoon, while it was employed on temporary duty drawing a hearse, the lifeboat signal sounded. The horse instinctively answered the call and was almost into the sea, coffin and all, before it was halted.

In the heart of the village stands a memorial statue to three lifeboatmen lost in 1916, an event still strong in local memory. Walter Grove and his son Courtney, lifeboatmen both, marvelled at the courage of the men who manned the boat. 'My grandfather was home on leave from the trenches,' Courtney said, 'but he didn't hesitate to man the lifeboat that day, exchanging one hell for another. That storm in 1916 was the worst in living memory. They were men of steel in those days.'

You don't travel far in Gower without encountering history's smugglers and pirates along the way. Robert Lucas, descendant of an old Gower family, met me at a sixteenth-century building in Port-Eynon and told me of its connection with his ancestor, John Lucas. This man was reputed to be a Bristol Channel pirate who, in Robin Hood fashion, supported his people with the profits of his piracy. The building has now been identified as an Elizabethan salt factory: you can see where seawater was heated and the salt extracted. But musket loopholes have also been found, lending credence to the story that the salt house was also the fortress-home of the pirate king.

After a scramble over the rocky beach I came to one of Gower's great mysteries, Culver Hole. A deep cleft in the cliff has been filled with a stone wall, pierced by four windows, as if a tower has been squashed in a vice of rocks.

Who built it? Pirates, smugglers? It seems unlikely. Looking at it, I reflected that smugglers would not have built such a large,

Culver Hole: the enduring mystery of Gower

substantial and permanent hide-out. Some think it was a pigeon loft built to keep up the supply of pigeon pies; but to my mind it is too remote and unlikely a spot for such a structure.

A stout rope, slightly frayed at the end like a lion's tail, dangled from the entrance which was twenty feet or so above my head. There was nothing for it. Up the rope I went, glad I had eaten that laverbread for breakfast. Feeling slightly as if I were in a schoolboy adventure yarn, I hauled myself into a dank, dark and eerie chamber which smelt of seaweed. Some broken, slippery steps led upwards and petered out. Like many others before me, I looked for clues which might have suggested the tower's purpose. There was no answer to the enigma. Theories flow in and out like the tide – and Culver Hole guards its secrets.

The path took me over the cliffs of the cave country and around gullies with colourful names – Groaning Slad, Red Gut, Yellow Top, Black Hole Gut. The cliff edges were embroidered with those lovely flowers, squill and thrift. Thrift, many will remember, was the flower on the old threepenny coins. The rocks below have worked like tin openers on the hulls of doomed ships. Once, a ship ran aground with a cargo of elephant tusks, a fortune in ivory, and all spirited away by locals.

Paviland Cave: sensational find astonished scientists

The walking was arduous in places. In the company of Dr Stephen Aldhouse-Green, an archaeologist, I picked my way down a gully to Paviland Cave, accessible for only a few hours between tides.

'A place of world-wide importance,' Stephen said, as we scrambled into the entrance. Here in 1823 Dr William Buckland, a geology professor from Oxford, found the prehistoric skeleton known as the Red Lady. It was later determined that the bones were those of a man aged about twenty, 5 feet 7 inches tall, but because they were buried with perforated seashells and ivory ornaments Buckland was at first persuaded that they were female.

The young man had been given a ceremonial burial and the bones had been stained with red ochre. For Christian fundamentalists like Buckland, who believed in the Biblical story of the Creation, the ancient bones, lying as they did among the remnants of long-extinct animals, posed difficult questions. Buckland suggested that the Red Lady had been buried in Roman times and that the animal bones had been swept into the cave in the Biblical Deluge. We now know that the Paviland skeleton is more than eighteen thousand years old; and, as Stephen told me, with careful digging and sifting the cave can still reveal clues to the early inhabitants of Gower.

Worm's Head: a serpent made of rock

High on the cliffs, I strode towards Worm's Head. It's nothing like a worm, of course: its old name means dragon and you can imagine it rearing from the sea. The ebbing tide uncovers a causeway enabling people to walk to the Head; but visitors are often marooned when the sea sweeps back. Len Beynon told me that low tide reveals a kingdom of succulent crabs and lobsters. 'The men who go crabbing keep the secrets of the good places. The knowledge is sacrosanct, passed down through the families.'

My goal, the terminus of my walk, was the village of Rhossili. Although modern transport makes it easy to reach, the village retains the feel of a lonely outpost. A plot in the churchyard is called Sailors' Corner, having been set aside in the last century for the corpses of seamen cast ashore on the sands. It says something about the dangers of the seafaring life that in a single month in 1844 twelve bodies were washed up here.

A plaque in the church provides a link with one of the defining British dramas, Captain Scott's Antarctic expedition of 1912. One of those who stood with Scott at the South Pole and perished on the terrible return journey was Chief Petty Officer Edgar Evans, who was born in Rhossili. Dedicating the plaque during a moving ceremony, the vicar said: 'There he lies, amid the eternal ice, a monument of courage.'

Looking out over the shining yellow sands I could see the protruding black bones of the *Helvetia*, wrecked here more than a century ago. Her mate, a handsome young Norwegian, stayed in Rhossili for some months and fell in love with a local girl, as sailors do. Her father, the story goes, refused her permission to marry him. She remained a spinster all her days. Perhaps she saw the wrecked ship, gradually eroded by the constant sea, as a memorial to a lost love.

I sat on the cliff for a while, enjoying the fading light of the day, just a little reluctant to bring to an end an absorbing walk. I vowed to repeat it as soon as I could.

The wreck of the *Helvetia*: a poignant story

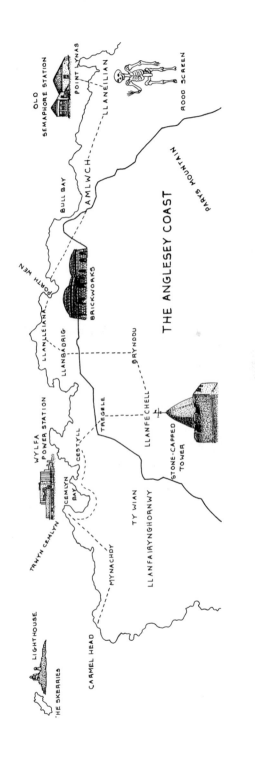

THE SKERRIES

LIGHTHOUSE

CARMEL HEAD

MYNACHDY

LLANFAIRYNGHORNWY

TY WIAN

TRWYN CEMLYN

CEMLYN BAY

CESTYLL

WYLFA POWER STATION

STONE-CAPPED TOWER

LLANFECHELL

TREGELE

BRYNDDU

LLANBADRIG

LLANLLEIANA

PORTH WEN

BRICKWORKS

BULL BAY

AMLWCH

LLANEILIAN

POINT LYNAS

OLD SEMAPHORE STATION

ROOD SCREEN

PARYS MOUNTAIN

THE ANGLESEY COAST

2. THE ANGLESEY COAST

An airplane eaten by a pig

A cold wind blew out of the north, tugging at my jacket, and dark scowling clouds were in the offing. It was not the best time to walk the craggy crescent at the top of Anglesey. But there were some scraps of blue sky for encouragement: all the makings, I thought, of a Jekyll and Hyde sort of day.

I have a particular liking for coastal walks. The moods of the sea compete with the grandeur of the land. Since this stretch of coast lies on the shipping route to Liverpool, a large part of its story is concerned with lighthouses, signalling, shipwrecks and lifeboats.

Appropriately, then, I started by the lighthouse at Point Lynas. Grey waves surged and exploded on the rocks below. The gleaming wet thread of the path stretched across the cliffs towards the west. To the south lay Dulas Island, its round tower built and stocked with provisions by a charitable Victorian squire as a shelter for shipwreck survivors; though the food was sometimes pilfered by fishermen.

Point Lynas and distant Dulas Island

On the hill above me rose an old semaphore station. Gwilym Jones, an historian I consulted about it, told me that in the 1820s ten of these were built on high points between Holyhead and Liverpool, relaying shipping news and weather messages by means of semaphore arms on tall masts. In fine weather it was very efficient: it took under five minutes for a signal to be transmitted from Holyhead to shipping agents and owners waiting in Liverpool for news of their ships and cargoes. A rather troublesome semaphore clerk received a message one day addressed to himself. It said: 'You are dismissed.'

The old semaphore station: here is the news

I felt like a galleon in a gale, whipped by the rain and blown along the path to the fifteenth-century church at Llaneilian. Not surprisingly, it guards the graves of many shipwrecked men.

The church is full of treasures. The most striking is the carved oak rood screen, five centuries old, with a grim figure of a skeleton warning of the wages of sin. On the other hand, the gaudily-painted figures of bagpipers in the chancel have nothing to do with religious solemnity and everything to do with dancing and enjoyment at festival time. A real curiosity are the stout wooden dog tongs, clearly dated 1748. There are only seven other sets surviving in Wales. John Owen Hughes told me about them.

The screen at Llaneilian Church...

'Shepherd boys used to take their dogs to church and if the sermon went on too long they mischievously encouraged their dogs to fight and bark. The churchwarden used the tongs to grasp the dogs by the neck and throw them out.'

A narrow passage leads to a little chapel where there is a wooden altar, half-rotted by time. It was once at the heart of a curious superstition. People believed that if they crawled through one of the narrow archways into the altar, turned around three times, and emerged from another arch they would be cured of sickness or be sure to live another year. I wondered what happened if people got stuck. Anyway, the church authorities installed panels to block the arches and stop the superstitious nonsense and, no doubt, the unseemly hilarity.

Back on the cliff path I came to a bizarre example of Welsh voodoo, the Cursing Well. If you wanted an enemy cursed you wrote his name on a slate and put it into the well. Some years ago a slate was found in the well with a little wax figure stuck to it, presumably the target of the curse. The victim, supposing he knew, paid the guardian of the well to remove the slate and lift the curse.

All the way into Amlwch I had an exhilarating walk, watching the waves rear up and hurl themselves against the cliffs. In snug Amlwch port, where yachts and fishing boats were sheltering, I talked to a skipper of one of the pilot cutters based here. The cutters are built for rough

... and the Cursing Well nearby

weather and are there to embark and disembark Liverpool pilots. If, because of bad weather, a pilot aboard an outward bound vessel cannot be taken off, he will have to be landed at Falmouth; and if not there he faces the prospect of an unscheduled trip to North or South America. I mused, on that stormy day, that I wouldn't mind 'rolling down to Rio'.

Copper Klondike: Parys Mountain

Amlwch was a wild place in its eighteenth and nineteenth-century heyday. It made its living from the copper quarries at Parys Mountain, two miles south of the town, where copper had been worked since Roman times. As a port and rail head, it thrived for a hundred years. With more than sixty pubs and the toughest miners whooping it up and lacing their beer with gunpowder, it could make a passable imitation of Dodge City. In 1900 it was observed that 'only the uncouth, the foolhardy and the brave' went out in Amlwch on Saturday night. Miners and sailors, and some-times their women, brawled in the streets and one of the notorious toughs, Dic Canaan, sharpened his clogs to a point. As a counter-balance to the pubs there were numerous Sunday schools; but there must have been occasions when the Almighty despaired of the town.

I knew nothing about the redoubtable 'copper ladies' of Anglesey, but Mair Williams, who is descended from one, served me tea and cake and entertained me with their remarkable story. The copper ladies (or laddies, as the word is pronounced locally), were the tough women who broke up the copper ore with hammers. They sang as they worked, not because they were happy, but because they liked to set up a rhythm as they steadily reduced the copper mountain to little pieces. By the standards of the times they were fairly well paid, women of some substance, independent and not at all compliant; and the men who married them had to be strong characters. Mrs Williams showed me a pair of wooden clogs worn by one of the copper ladies. The acid in the environment in which they worked rotted ordinary shoes.

In the copper epoch, Amlwch had a thriving tobacco trade. John Jones, who joined Morgans, his family's tobacco business, in 1939, told me that Amlwch had three tobacco companies making shag and twist tobacco, both for smoking and, in places where naked lights were forbidden, for chewing. Morgan brands included Yr Hen Wlad, Baco'r Byd, Baco Aelwyd and Taffy Twist which sold for eightpence or tenpence an ounce. The dull job of packing was done by four teenage girls. The business declined and finally ended in 1985. John Jones told me, with a laugh, that local farmers swore that there was nothing better for de-worming a horse than an ounce of Amlwch shag pushed down the wretched animal's throat.

The route took me through quiet Bull Bay. With a raven croaking and nagging at me as I pushed through the jungle of ferns growing over the path, I reached Porth Wen and descended the steep path leading to the abandoned brickworks which had prospered in the early years of the century. The sea was crashing into the little harbour. The interesting buildings here are the domed kilns which look a little like small red-brick mosques. I had the bonus of sunshine as I continued to Llanlleiana; and the rare thrill of watching a peregrine falcon, that brilliant

The old brickworks at Porth Wen

hunter, swooping low over the cliff top.

I felt that I was swooping myself as I rounded the curve of the coast and came to Llanbadrig church, a simple and pretty place whose roots can be traced to the fifth century. The story has it that it was founded by St Patrick who was wrecked on the Middle Mouse rock a short distance offshore and found refuge in a cave. The lovely sanctuary tiles in the church are of glass, of the distinctive blue that I have seen in mosques in central Asia, especially those in Samarkand. They were installed during the 1884 restoration which was paid for by the diplomat Lord Stanley of Alderley. He had embraced Islam and insisted on an Islamic flavour to the church. He had, incidentally, married his Spanish wife in four separate religious ceremonies, only to discover that she had a husband still living.

Turning inland, I made for Llanfechell. The stone cap on the church tower was placed by a squire to quieten the bells which, he said, were disturbing his bees. The village was the home of John Elias, the most famous Methodist preacher of the early nineteenth century, so stern and implacable he seemed carved from rock and was known as the Methodist pope. The staple diet and the rise of the chapels led to the comment that Anglesey's story could be told

Muffling the bells of Llanfechell Church

29

in two words: oats and Methodism.

Brynddu, a large and handsome house near Llanfechell, was the home of Squire William Bulkeley. From 1734 until his death in 1760 he kept a vividly-written diary, an absorbing picture of Anglesey life before the chapels took a grip. The squire wrote, among other things, about the wild football games played by the youths of neighbouring parishes. There were barely any rules and the teams consisted of scores of young men. They rampaged over the countryside, the goalposts being the porches of Llanfechell and Llanbadrig churches.

Bill Grove-White, the owner of Brynddu, showed me the house's massive beams. 'Tropical hardwood,' he said, adding that they may have come from a Spanish Armada ship wrecked on the Anglesey coast. He showed me, too, his painting of the ship *Fame*, captained by the privateer Fortunatus Wright who seduced, and in 1738 married, Squire Bulkeley's daughter, Mary. His days of preying on French ships ended when he was drowned in the Mediterranean in 1756.

At Maes Mawr farm near Llanfechell, farmer Tom Jones took his hammer to chip off some samples of the green and purple rock, popular in the nineteenth century, that used to be known as Mona Marble. The fashionable designer George Bullock bought the quarry here and used the 'marble' stone in the furniture he made for his wealthy London clients.

I walked up the road to Cromlech farm, which harbours a story of treachery. The version I heard, and there are variations, was that in the 1640s the young owner of the farm was engaged to a local girl, but, being on the King's side in the Civil War, fled to France when the Roundheads won. He returned unexpectedly. Next day he galloped his horse off a cliff. His last letter explained it all. The young man's brother had written to him in France saying: 'Don't come home, your fiancée is dead and the Roundheads have seized the land.' In fact, the brother had grabbed the farm and married the girl. The suicide note concluded: 'My cup overflows with bitterness.'

From Tregele I made my way across the fields to the shore. I had permission to visit Cestyll, an almost secret garden of rocks, water and shrubs, lovingly developed in the 1920s by the Honourable Violet Vivian, whose ashes are scattered here. The garden is open to the public on one day a year.

A rare treat: the gardens at Cestyll

I rounded the coast into Cemlyn Bay and tramped the shingle beach beside the bird sanctuary, my ears filled with the chatter of hundreds of nesting terns in the lagoon. The sanctuary was started in 1930 by Vivian Hewitt, a reclusive millionaire and devoted ornithologist who built his own refuge, Bryn Aber, the house concealed by high, grey, fortress-like walls at the end of the beach.

Hewitt was one of that brave breed, a pioneer aviator. On April 26 1912, aged twenty-four, he made the first flight from Holyhead to Dublin, a sixty-mile journey. Halfway across the Irish Sea in his Bleriot monoplane he ran into fog – and he had no compass. But before he entered the fog he had noted the angle of the sun on his wing and when he emerged he adjusted his course so that the sun fell at the same angle. He landed and asked two men: 'Where am I?' They told him: 'Phoenix Park, Dublin.'

Ann Farrell, whose father, William Hywel, a local doctor, wrote a book about him, told me that Hewitt loved birds so much he paid £5 for every cat brought to him. He eventually exiled himself to the Bahamas, to escape the taxman, taking with him his devoted housekeeper. But he returned to Wales towards the end of his life and died near his beloved bird sanctuary in 1965.

On the way out to the point of Trwyn Cemlyn I inspected the stone commemorating the first lifeboat in Anglesey. Kyffin Williams, the artist, who lives in Anglesey, told me the story. His great-grandfather, James Williams, and his great-grandmother, Frances, had watched horrified as a ship broke up on rocks and one hundred and thirty-three people drowned. They vowed to provide a lifeboat, raised the money and stationed it at Cemlyn, close to the Skerries rocks. Williams, who was rector of Llanfairynghornwy, became coxswain and was awarded a gold medal for one of his selfless deeds. His wife, equally courageous, sometimes took an active part in rescues. The Anglesey lifeboats saved more than four hundred lives before they were taken over by the Royal National Lifeboat Institution in 1856.

A good long stride brought me to Mynachdy farm, a monastery in the twelfth century, and the background of an extraordinary and romantic story. In 1745 a small boy, rescued from a shipwreck, was carried to Mynachdy and treated by Dr Lloyd, who lived nearby at Maes.

The boy, thought to be Spanish, was placed in the care of a farmer and given the name of Evan Thomas. The doctor played a part in his upbringing. It became clear that Evan was exceptionally gifted. As a boy he mended the broken leg of a chicken and treated other birds and animals; and thereafter demonstrated that with his sensitive touch, his intuition and skill as a manipulator, he was a natural bone-setter. People with fractures and dislocations sought him out and his fame as a healer spread. His four sons were similarly gifted; so were many other descendants. The Anglesey bone-setters became famous.

Evan Thomas's great-grandson, Hugh Owen Thomas, 1834-91, established a remarkable orthopaedic practice in Liverpool and invented the invaluable Thomas splint which was used to treat thousands of wounded soldiers in the First World War. His nephew, Sir Robert Jones, who started in medicine alongside his uncle Hugh, became the greatest orthopaedic surgeon of his day. His name endures in the famous Robert Jones and Agnes Hunt orthopaedic hospital at Gobowen, near Oswestry.

At the turn of the century, in the house called Ty Wian, across the fields, an old parchment was found in a wall on which was written some Welsh doggerel. One verse, in rough translation, went something like this:

Carts without horses soon we'll see.
Crashes in plenty then there'll be.
Thoughts across the world will fly
In the twinkling of an eye.
Above the clouds brave men will rise
And float in chariots across the skies.
Then the end of the world will come
In nineteen hundred and ninety-one!

The neighbouring farm to Mynachdy is Bryn Goelcerth, the stage on which Robert Loraine played his thrilling bit-part in the history of flying. Loraine was a leading London actor, a heart-throb of his day, and a daring and enthusiastic pilot, if not always a lucky one.

Roy Sloan, an aviation historian, told me his tale. In August 1910, planning to be the first to fly across the Irish Sea, Loraine set off across north Wales in his little Farman biplane, aiming for Holyhead. On his way he ran out of fuel and crash-landed in a field at Bryn Goelcerth. He repaired the plane but shortly after take-off crashed it on Mynachdy. He rebuilt his machine at Bryn Goelcerth, a task made more difficult when a pig ate part of the canvas fabric of a wing. Meanwhile, his young French mechanic's frolics with wine and village girls created a scandal among the chapel-minded locals.

Under the gaze of an excited crowd, Loraine took off again and

Carmel Head navigation beacons

promptly crashed. In never-say-die mood, he dusted himself down, loaded the pieces onto a wagon and reassembled them in Holyhead. At last, ever daring, he took off for Dublin but crashed into the sea a mile from the Irish coast. He swam ashore and made it back to London just in time to take the stage at the Haymarket Theatre in a play called *The Man From The Sea*.

The wind was still blowing hard, but I was enveloped in the glow of evening sunshine as I walked rapidly to Carmel Head, past the two tall white pyramid beacons used as navigation marks. From the headland I had a good view of the fearsome Skerries rocks and the lighthouse. It was the last privately-owned lighthouse in Britain and probably the richest. The original tower had a beacon fed by coal rowed out from the mainland, a laborious and costly business. Shipping in and out of Liverpool multiplied in the nineteenth century and, since the Skerries were on the route, the lighthouse was a vital navigation point. Indeed, for the lighthouse owners, the rocks themselves might have been of gold: they prospered mightily from the penny-a-ton duties collected from ships.

At last, after a long legal battle, Trinity House bought the light-house in 1841 for £444,984 11s 3d, an astonishing amount in those days. In the judgment of many people at the time it was a sum that stood as a testimony to the greed of the owners.

The Skerries lighthouse: a stormy saga

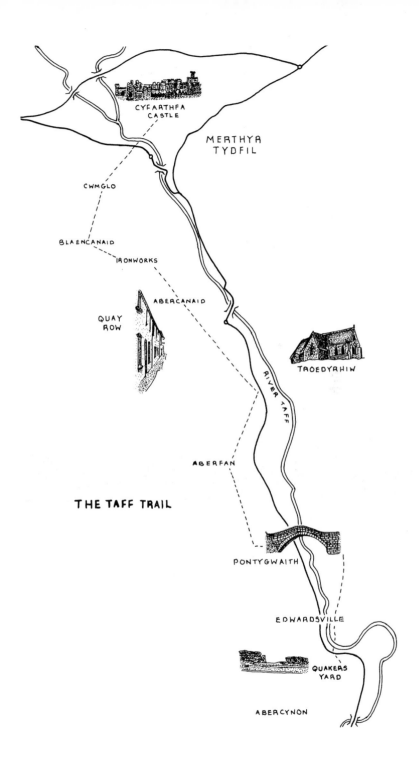

CYFARTHFA
CASTLE

MERTHYR
TYDFIL

CWMGLO

BLAENCANAID

IRONWORKS

ABERCANAID

QUAY
ROW

RIVER TAFF

TROEDYRHIW

ABERFAN

THE TAFF TRAIL

PONTYGWAITH

EDWARDSVILLE

QUAKERS
YARD

ABERCYNON

3. THE TAFF TRAIL

The land of anvils

Not so many years ago people would have given you a quizzical look had you told them you proposed walking the valley of the Taff up to Merthyr Tydfil. It was not just in English minds that the river, and its sister streams in the southern valleys, had an image of dark and bitter waters running through a battered black landscape.

Many of the scars of industry remain, the legacy of an astonishing history. Some of the industrial structures might strike you as brooding monuments; and parts of the landscape speak powerfully of hardship and suffering. Nature, in its kindly cosmetic way, has greened many places that were once ugly; and modern landscapers have removed tips and rubbish. Some ruins have been pulled down, a pity in certain cases, for they had stories to tell; but there is still much to see and to look for.

I'm enthralled by this countryside. It is one of history's crucibles, with the experiences of dramatic events and the sense of

Reformed character: the River Taff near Edwardsville

36

great arguments close at hand. The Taff Trail is an imaginative creation, running fifty-five miles from Cardiff to Brecon, and you can dip into it for a stride or a stroll.

To give myself a day's walk to Merthyr, I started at Quakers Yard, named after a Quaker burial ground. Walking on the west bank, I was soon on a broad path beneath the trees, the valley slopes blanketed with bluebells, sunlight flashing on the tumbling river. This was how Daniel Defoe saw the area in the 1720s ... 'A most agreeable vale with a pleasant river running through it called the Taafe.'

Before long, I was in the land of giants, muscular bridges and viaducts with an an imposing imperial feel to them, the majestic survivors of the volcanic age of iron and coal. Near Edwardsville the valley is at its narrowest and all the transport systems had to be squeezed into this narrow gorge. It was the vital conduit through which wealth, in the form of coal and iron, poured towards Cardiff and its docks and counting houses.

The greatest Victorian engineers, titans like Isambard Kingdom Brunel, demonstrated their genius and daring here. You stand in awe at what those frock-coated, cigar-chomping men achieved with

A giant's bite: Taff valley quarry

stone and iron. Within a space of fifty yards or so I passed by the remains of the railroads and viaducts that formed the busiest railway junction in the land. Such was the volume of traffic that one of the viaducts had to be doubled in size only twenty years after it was built. The Taff Vale railway, laid down in 1841, was the richest in the world and around here, labourers quarried relentlessly, hauling stone down the hill. I was filled with a thrilling sense of energy, of men wrestling the landscape in the age of industrial convulsion.

'Merthyr was where it was all happening,' Brian Davies, an historian, told me. 'It created Cardiff as a port and the Taff valley was the connection between Merthyr and Cardiff. It was the first valley to have a canal, in 1794; the first to have a railway, in 1841; and the site of an experiment with a tramway.'

Bolt-holes on Trevithick's tramway

My path followed the track of this tramway, built by the Cornish engineer Richard Trevithick in 1804. Some of the stones that held the rails in place are still there and I put my fingers into the bolt-holes, imagining the clanking and grinding of wheels. This is really the birthplace of railway transport. One of Merthyr's iron masters bet five hundred guineas that Trevithick's steam locomotive could haul five loaded wagons the nine miles to Abercynon. Its top speed was five miles an hour, not much faster than I could walk it, and the ironmaster won his bet. A pretty eighteenth-

Bridge-builder's art: Pontygwaith

century bridge spans the river at Pontygwaith, its graceful curves married to utility: it once gave access to an ironworks. I watched a fisherman casting for trout. The Taff, which once ran black, has cleared in the miracle of renewal; and the fish are prospering. Ray Pearce, who also fishes here, said that the deep, clean gravel beds in the river are ideal for salmon and that everyone who knew the river was excited by the prospect of salmon returning to spawn, making their way upriver by way of a fish pass.

I left the peaceful shadow-speckled path of the river gorge and walked through a tunnel under the new Cardiff to Merthyr highway. You have to endure some traffic noise for a while on this stretch. I reflected philosophically that the road is a blessing, freeing the valley from the tyranny of traffic congestion. Not so long ago, as many will remember, the narrow road to Merthyr had all the hardship of a pilgrim's penance. Aberfan is on the route, its name, unforgettable, indelible, encapsulating grief and anger at the cruellest blow, the loss of a generation of children. One hundred and sixteen children and twenty-eight adults died when the mountain of colliery waste fell on Pantglas school in October 1966. The inscriptions on the rows of white memorials remain infinitely moving. Aberfan was an ordinary mining village but its people showed extraordinary qualities. It would have been understandable had many of them wanted to get away from the place. In fact, most of the villagers stayed on and discovered strength, comfort and leadership. In the years after the disaster the anger of people in south Wales was converted into a determination to rid the valleys of their terrible wounds, to restore a former beauty through reclamation, landscaping and planting.

Pharaoh's tomb: Anthony Hill's church at Troedyrhiw

Along the road, in Troedyrhiw, I looked into the church built by Anthony Hill, one of the industrial heavyweights of Merthyr, master of the Plymouth ironworks. As a mark of his conceit, and power, he decreed that no-one but he should be buried here. The church is thus his mausoleum. David Evans, a local man who knows the story well, described for me the burial of this pharaoh of the valleys. 'It was in 1862. He was put in a coffin of elm, lined with Welsh flannel. That was placed inside a casket of lead, and that in turn was enclosed in an oak coffin and placed on an oak plinth.'

The modern footpath runs for a while along the bed of the old canal. In its day it was the most profitable waterway on earth, a vital artery whose forty-nine locks in twenty-four miles were open twenty-four hours a day. It made so much money that it had to reduce its tolls and for part of a year, in 1816-17, charged nothing at all. It was in use until 1915, when its banks burst. Thereafter its cargoes went by rail.

I felt an almost gravitational pull as I approached Merthyr, as if it were waiting to tell its epic story. In the gardens on the outskirts I saw the first monkey puzzle trees of my walk. These were a Victorian middle-class status symbol. For some reason you often see them in the gardens of Nonconformist clergy.

At Abercanaid I left the Taff trail for a while and walked onto the old coal workings above Gethin farm. The ruins of the nineteenth-century colliery stood here until the 1970s but were demolished, for fear that they might prove dangerous, in the aftermath of Aberfan. A concrete cap covers the shaft and I pushed a stone through a hole and listened as it fell 188 yards to make an echoing splash at the bottom.

Disaster site: old coal workings, Abercanaid

Stephen Richards, a local historian who guided me to the ruins, described the disaster of 1862 when forty-seven men were killed in an explosion. 'There were two shafts and at the bottom of one burned an open fire which drew in cold air through a second shaft. This was for ventilation. But the fire ignited the gases. The lesson was not learnt. Three years later the same thing happened and thirty-five were killed.'

Back on the trail I stood on the slope where thousands gathered in 1847 to witness the first balloon flight over Merthyr. The gallant aeronaut took off but reckoned without the hot blast from the Plymouth ironworks: he shot high into the sky and did not come down until Quakers Yard.

Quay Row, Abercanaid: boots on the cobbles

Walking by the whitewashed cottages at Quay Row in Abercanaid I found it easy enough to imagine the hobnailed boots marching the well-trodden cobbles; and the street name is a reminder that the canal ran near here. The house behind the row, with its monkey puzzle tree in the garden, of course, was the birthplace of William Thomas Lewis, who went to work at thirteen as an engineering apprentice. He later became Lord Merthyr, last of the great coal tycoons, a hard-headed leader of the coal owners, a pitiless opponent of the miners and 'the best hated man' in Wales in the 1890s and the early years of the century. His statue stands at Merthyr Hospital.

I headed up into the land that made Merthyr rich and mighty. Here men found all they needed for industrial power: iron ore and coal, timber, limestone and abundant water. Every inch, it seems, was ransacked for minerals, and every ounce of wealth carted away. There is a strong sense of the land being squeezed and sucked dry. Some of it has the tortured appearance of an old battlefield.

Abandoned ironworks: reclaimed by the trees

A climb up the steep mountainside brought me to a wooded area, about a mile above Merthyr, which conceals the most evocative and substantial monuments to the town's past. Broken mossy steps took me through the centuries into a green glade and the massive and overgrown ruins of an ironworks. They brought to mind the temple ruins I have seen in Mexico raised to gods all-powerful and relentlessly demanding. I felt like an explorer in a lost civilisation. Here among the brambles and trees I imagined the clamour of the ironworks, the roaring of furnaces and shouts and curses of men, the whinnying of horses, the searing heat and acrid fumes.

But men were making iron in this district long before Merthyr sprang into explosive life. There was plenty of timber that could be rendered into charcoal and the iron ore lay close to the surface. Not far from the ruins, beside a spring and a rusty pool, I examined a sixteenth-century furnace, in which the molten deposits of iron could still be seen.

If Merthyr was made by iron, it was also made by faith. In this region iron – and society itself – were put to the anvil. I walked the hillside above Blaencanaid farm where the first congregations of religious dissenters met in fearful conclave. Before the Toleration Acts of 1689 it was dangerous to practice dissent. One day the authorities fell on Blaencanaid farm, arrested twenty-four worshippers and hustled them to jail.

Secret prayers: ruined chapel at Cwmglo

Around here, dissent bubbled like a spring. In the years that followed it became a river. Part of the story can be found in the evocative ruined chapel at Cwmglo. It is a secret place some distance from Merthyr – and, as I discovered, still hard to find. At a time when new ideas of religion and society were taking hold and challenging the established order, Nonconformists put down a tentative root here. In 1739 the Methodist pioneer Howell Harris came to preach. The people who gathered at Cwmglo and other places were the radicals, the dissenters who shaped Merthyr and its political tradition. Their independent religious thought turned into an independent political outlook.

There was another Merthyr, too, volatile, dark, lurid and diseased. 'A vision of Hell,' noted Thomas Carlyle in 1850. 'All cinders, and dust-mounds and soot'. In one of the novels of Anthony Trollope a young curate, told he is being posted to Merthyr, faints away.

The town had its ugliest expression in the sprawling district known as China. 'It was the worst slum in Merthyr, itself a collection of slums,' said Keith Strange, an historian with a particular interest in the place and the period. 'A warren of hovels, filth and brothels – and overlords who ran the crime networks in the valleys, all the way down to the ports. China flourished from the 1820s to the 1870s, coinciding with the boom in the iron industry, and was ruled by criminal potentates who styled themselves emperors.'

Some of these 'emperors' were transported to Australia. One of them, Ben Richards, on trial at Merthyr, shouted a speech to his excited fans. 'They may transport me or hang me,' he said in a show of bravado, 'but I'll die like a chip!' – meaning he would stay cheerful to the end.

For more than sixty years Merthyr was the largest town in Wales, the largest iron and steel manufacturer on earth. And above the teeming human anthill lived the ironmasters. The greatest were the Crawshays, a dynasty founded by the Yorkshire colossus Richard Crawshay who bought the Cyfarthfa ironworks in 1794

Cyfarthfa: iron king's castle

and grew rich on the wars with France. The rotund, John Bull-like Crawshay glowed with pride on the day in 1802 that Lord Nelson visited the ironworks to see for himself where the navy's cannon and cannonballs were made.

The emotional Crawshay presented the admiral to a huge crowd of workers. 'Here's your Nelson, boys,' he bellowed, 'so shout, you buggers, shout.' And shout they did; and Nelson, who had a flair for public relations, gave a guinea to the first man to toast his health in Welsh.

The Crawshay dynasty bestrode Merthyr for a century, their story such a saga of power, wealth and eccentricity that it reads like the stuff of a blockbuster novel. All the Crawshay men quarrelled bitterly with their fathers. It was Richard Crawshay's grandson, William, who in 1825 built Cyfarthfa Castle, with its 365 rooms, a symbol of luxury and power. William's son Robert, an obsessed and difficult man, took a virulent dislike to a church in the town and ordered that it be hidden from his view by coal tips. 'He had become a crabby old man,' Margaret Paine explained to me when I visited the church, 'and his family had left him. He said he would bury the church and he almost did: the tips were all around it.'

The old Court of Requests

Meanwhile, fierce political passions grew and then exploded. The Chartists came to Merthyr, demanding political reform. I enjoyed a drink at the Three Horseshoes and the licensee, Mary Hovarth, showed me the room where Chartists crammed themselves in for meetings. 'The Home Secretary sent a spy called William Griffith to infiltrate the meetings and report back to him,' she said. You can still read his reports in the public records.

Close by is another pub, with the curious name of the Court of Requests, which was the debtors' court in the 1830s. A crowd of revolutionaries stormed it before seizing the town, raising the red flag and holding out for three days before soldiers came in force to restore order. Somehow the thrill and the pride remain fresh. Dr Elwyn Bowen, who has a fine view of Merthyr from his home, told me that his great-grandfather, Dafydd Lewis, was wounded by soldiers in June 1831 and made his way home, a musket ball in his shoulder. 'An army surgeon was informed that there was a wounded rioter, went to the house and removed the musket ball. While he was there, rioters surrounded the house, took the surgeon to some waste ground, removed his sword and were ready to shoot him. But Dafydd Lewis came out and pleaded for the man's life. The rioters let the surgeon go. And as he waved his cockaded hat they fired their guns above his head.'

In its time Merthyr was legendary, a furnace where political and religious passions met red-hot iron. In its ascendancy and in its long and wretched decline, it played a large part in the story of Wales and of Britain. Few towns, I reflected as I ended my walk, have such a rumbustious history.

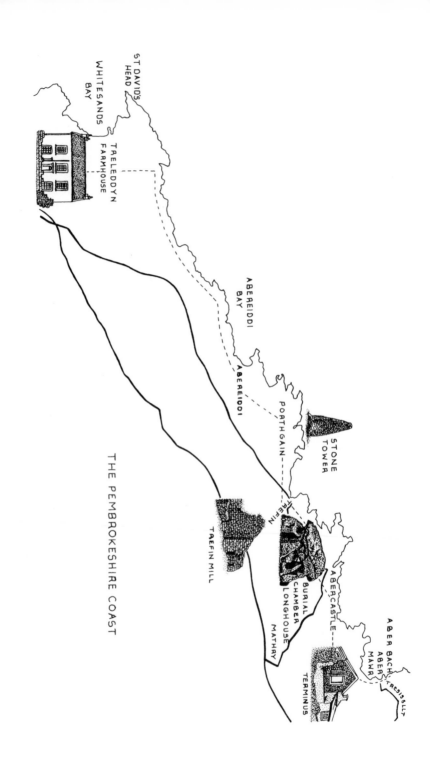

THE PEMBROKESHIRE COAST

ST DAVIDS HEAD

WHITESANDS BAY

TRELEDDYN FARMHOUSE

ABEREIDDI BAY

ABEREIDDI

PORTHGAIN

STONE TOWER

TREFIN

TAEFIN MILL

BURIAL CHAMBER

LONGHOUSE

MATHRY

ABERCASTLE

TERMINUS

ABER BACH

ABER MAWR

TRESISSLLT

4. THE PEMBROKESHIRE COAST

The path to the painted ceiling

Over the years I've travelled several stretches of the Pembrokeshire coast, enjoying its nobility, drama and diversity. The coastal footpath is a marvel, snaking 168 miles from the Teifi estuary to Amroth – and one of my ambitions is to walk every yard of it.

For our *Wild Tracks* journey I set out on an east to west route, from Aber Bach to Whitesands Bay, near St David's Head, a path well-ornamented with curiosities and with wonderful views every step of the way.

From my clifftop starting point I watched a patrolling customs vessel heading up the coast. It was a mile offshore, its bow plunging like a piston in and out of the swell. With all the aids of modern science its crew was continuing a battle that has not changed much in essentials for hundreds of years. With its numerous little coves, Pembrokeshire is ideal for smugglers. In the old days they brought in brandy. These days the cargoes are drugs. Keith Dufton, an ex-coastguard, told me about the time, a few years ago, when customs men swooped on a smuggling gang at Aber Bach. 'An inflatable boat was seen disappearing into a cave and we went off to find it. I lowered my son down, with a customs officer, and they found a cargo of cannabis worth £4,000,000.'

Wrecks and smugglers

49

Smugglers, high drama, treasure on the beach: Aber Bach has had them all. Tom Bennett, who has made a study of wrecks along this coast, told me about the terrific storm of 1859 which destroyed nine ships along the coast from Cardigan to St David's and drowned forty men. A wooden chest of coins was washed up on Aber Bach beach and carried off by a small boy. A farmer who saw him had a shrewd idea that the chest contained treasure, gave the lad a shilling for it and sent him on his way. That night a servant girl at the farm heard the chink of coins and, looking through the floorboards, saw the farmer counting out gold sovereigns on the kitchen table. He later used them to buy land.

Aber Bach Cove

Like any self-respecting Welsh cove, Aber Bach has a story of a comely mermaid. Romeo Colella, a young man who was born nearby, in the farm at Tresissllt, explained to me that he had good reason to know the tale. More than two centuries ago, the farmer here found the mermaid on the beach and took her to his home. Angry, and missing the sea, she cursed the farm, declaring that any child born there would not live beyond infancy. 'Strangely enough,' said Romeo, 'no child was born on the farm for two hundred and fifty years. As far I know, I'm the first.'

On the wild headland between Aber Bach and Aber Mawr, I came to a sturdy white cottage which was the humble terminus of the first transatlantic telegraph cable, the grandfather of them all. A cable was laid from here to Ireland in 1862, and, four years later, in an epic operation, Isambard Kingdom Brunel's steamship *Great Eastern* laid a cable from Ireland to Heart's Content in Newfoundland.

End of the line: terminus of telegraph cable to Ireland

Some years earlier, Brunel, of the ever-fertile imagination, had grand designs on obscure little Aber Mawr. Roger Worsley, who has investigated the history, told me that Brunel planned a large ocean terminal for his own steamships with a considerable manufacturing town alongside it. 'Just think,' said Roger, 'it could have been another Liverpool.' But the dream died and the only evidence of what might have been is a railway embankment.

The cliff path took me along the edge, between land, sea and sky. It was spring and the cliff flowers were out on parade. For music I had the seething sea. To my left was the village of Mathry, the birthplace of John Brown Evans, believed locally to be the inventor of a device that was both beneficial and horrific.

As a young man he quarrelled with his father and sailed for South Africa: isn't it amazing how many Victorian adventure stories begin with a young man stomping off in a huff? Anyway, he became a farmer in his new homeland; and, to control his stock, invented Evans Patent Fencing, more popularly known as barbed

wire. In its various forms, barbed wire revolutionised land management on the world's frontiers. In America, for example, it did far
more than Samuel Colt's revolver to tame the Wild West. And, of
course, it was used to terrible effect in war.

The path took me into the village of Abercastle, where there
used to be shops, pubs and shipbuilding yards. Its small harbour
was a welcome refuge in a storm. It was certainly a haven for a
remarkable twenty-four-year-old American, Alfred Johnson, who,
on August 10 1876, sailed in at the helm of his eighteen-foot dory.
To the astonishment of the local people he announced that he had
been at sea forty-six days, having sailed from Gloucester,
Massachusetts. His boat had no cabin and he had survived a
capsize in mid-Atlantic. After only two days' rest he asked direc-
tions and sailed off to Liverpool. He must have been a man of giant
spirit. I felt there should be a piece of inscribed granite at
Abercastle to record his epic voyage.

Carreg Sampson: cromlech near Longhouse Farm

The settlers who arrived in west Wales five thousand years ago
have left us the remains of their burial chambers to ponder on. At
Longhouse Farm the path took me by one of the more spectacular of these dolmens (cromlechau in Welsh) and led me to wonder
by what means the massive capstone was lifted onto the seven
uprights; and what sort of faith inspired the people in their labours.

After-dinner inspiration: Trefin Mill

The ruins of the corn mill at Trefin are evocative. Most Welsh-speakers know the lovely poem written about it by William Crwys Williams, three times an Eisteddfod Crown winner. One evening in 1918, after supper, he walked to the mill, sat in thought, then walked home, thinking hard. The dinner plates were still on the table. Did he wash up? No. Real poets don't wash up. He pushed the plates aside, took up his pen and wrote his famous lines, saying that the mill at Trefin, on the sea's edge, had ground its last corn, the last pony had turned for home with the last load, and now the mill itself was being worn down by time and the relentless wind.

The stubby digit of a stone tower on the cliff beckoned me to Porthgain, the most dramatic harbour on this stretch of the coast and a most remarkable industrial ruin and monument. Porthgain granite was used to build the Tate Gallery in London and in the construction of many buildings in Dublin. It was also employed extensively as the solid bed of city tramways, so that Porthgain boomed in the heyday of the trams. The quarry here was worked into the 1930s. The rock was crushed and shovelled into huge storage hoppers and loaded into sailing vessels and steamers which waited in queues outside the bottleneck harbour entrance.

This way: the beacon above Porthgain

Getting into the port was a formidable test of seamanship: and I could see quite clearly that for a sailing ship there was no second chance. In the Sloop Inn, a lively focus of village life, there hangs the carved stern section of the *Carolina* which ran into Porthgain in a great storm. The ship was being blown towards the rocks and the narrow entrance of Porthgain offered the only hope. The captain judged it with skill and a cool nerve, steering through the roaring sea, smashing into the jetty. All thirteen men aboard survived, scrambling over the bowsprit to safety.

The walls of the bar are like a museum, a sort of ledger telling the story of Porthgain's industry and of the ships that jostled for attention in the tiny harbour. Over his pint and a pipe, Merfyn

Sea drama: Porthgain Harbour

Saved from the wreck: carved stern section of the *Carolina*

Jones told me about his seagoing days. 'I went to sea at fourteen on a ship taking Welsh steam coal to Buenos Aires. I was the galley boy, peeling potatoes from morning to night. We waited for three months for a crop of corn to grow and I thought I'd never see Porthgain again. And when I saw that little stack above the harbour I said that's the end of seagoing for me.' Nevertheless, he earned much of his living at sea.

Porthgain people feel very strongly about their village. When

Abereiddi with its shipping beacon

the quarry owners put the houses up for sale in 1981 the villagers clubbed together and raised £55,000 to buy them. The celebration party has gone down in local history.

The coastal path follows every sinuous twist and rocky wrinkle. The inherent drama in the walk is the contrast between the pastoral peacefulness of the land and the endless combat between the sea and the jagged rocks. I came to Abereiddi which has an entrancing aquamarine lagoon. It once flourished as a slate quarry. The tower on the headland was a shipping beacon; though I like the fanciful story that it was the slate company boardroom and the place where the directors' wives had their afternoon tea.

There's little left of the village. It suffered two devastating blows in the 1930s, a giant wave followed by an outbreak of disease. Granville Phillips, who lived there, has the starkest memories of what happened.

'I was seven years old. There was a terrific storm and my father got us out of bed and carried us outside. I remember how frightened I was by the roaring of the sea. Then the village was hit by typhoid and that put the cap on it. We were completely isolated. If you wanted bread or coal you put the money on the ground because people did not want to touch you. We were like lepers. The village was finished. I can never get over it.'

The cemented roofs of cottages in these parts are typical of Pembrokeshire. In the old days the slates were of such poor quality that a thick coat of cement was applied to render them waterproof; and this method is still used today in some cases, in keeping with tradition.

Suddenly, as I walked on, the landscape seemed to empty. There was no farm in sight, no village, no harbour. I had the cliffs to myself. I came across some rather mysterious hand-printed signs on a fence. They directed me to Maes-y-Mynydd and another sign pointed to Claddfa, a burial place. But there was no village, only fallen stones overgrown with thistles and brambles.

I heard the story of the place from Glyn Griffiths, who lives nearby, and is passionate about it. Many of the people who lived here were Quakers, farm workers who had hard and uncertain lives and ached for a new life in America. 'They called their meeting place New York Cottage and gave the name New York Road to the lane that runs through the village. Somehow, I feel that their spirit is still alive. I feel I know them. They were born in poverty and died in poverty; and the church, though it was rich and powerful, did nothing to help them, to its everlasting shame and damnation.'

I walked down New York Road and left the ghosts of Maes-y-Mynydd to their yearning.

Maes-y-Mynydd: 'shame and damnation'

For a while the path is like a parapet, high above the sea, and then it threads through a lovely valley to Whitesands Bay. I inspected the stone that marks the place where St Patrick, one of that considerable army of roving Welsh saints, set off to take Christianity to Ireland.

Faith was only one of the reasons why men sailed for Ireland in cockleshell boats. Others, more materialistic, went for the copper and gold that lay in the Wicklow hills. When they returned with their treasure it sometimes slipped through their fingers into the unforgiving sand. How do we know? Because, thanks to patience and science, the sand now gives up its stories. Roy Lewis, who describes himself as a metal detectorist, has spent many nose-numbing hours sweeping the beach with his metal detector, concentrating on the sound in his earphones. He showed me some of the treasures he has found: Viking coins, axe heads from the Bronze Age and a little nugget of Irish gold for which men risked the sea. 'The best time for prospecting,' Roy said, 'is after the severe winter storms which uncover the beaches.'

The white Georgian farmhouse at Treleddyn marked the finishing post of my walk. It has more than its fair share of history. One stormy day in the 1760s, the remarkable Mrs Blanch Williams, the farmer's wife, looked out to sea through a telescope and saw seven shipwrecked men crawling on the rocks some miles offshore. Nona Rees, who told me the story, said that Mrs Williams launched a small boat with a sail and oars and 'set out across one of the wickedest stretches of water in Britain'. She plucked the men from the rocks, brought them to safety and looked after them at Treleddyn. They were Swedish seamen and, when they returned home, they gratefully set up a stone recording Mrs Williams's courage.

In 1797 her widower Thomas was walking on these cliffs when he saw some ships. He did not like the look of them, even though they were flying British colours. He followed them up the coast, telling everyone that he feared they were French. He was right. They landed troops at Carregwastad on Strumble Head, the notorious last invasion of Britain.

A frequent visitor at Treleddyn was Mrs Williams's cousin, Grace, who had a daughter, Dora, born 1761, who also stayed here. As Dora Jordan she became the greatest comedy star of her day. Crowds flocked to theatres to see her. One admirer was William, Duke of Clarence, the future King William IV. She became his devoted mistress, bore him ten children, the

Treleddyn Farmhouse... royal romance

FitzClarences, and gave him a happily fulfilling family life for twenty years, though newspapers and caricaturists cruelly satirised the affair. She could not, of course, become his wife. The happy relationship ended and Dora went to Paris where she died, heart-broken, in 1816. The remorseful King William commissioned Sir Francis Chantrey, the greatest sculptor of his day, to carve a life-size statue of her. It is now in Buckingham Palace. I encountered Sir Francis's work again, during my walk through the Ystwyth Valley.

There is a tradition that Dora and the Duke used to meet in Wales. Indeed, the story goes that Dora and the Duke spent bliss-ful hours in a bedroom at Treleddyn. I climbed the stairs to this room and, naturally enough, looked at the ceiling, for it is part of the story that, perhaps as a delicious expression of the lovers' inti-mate humour, the Duke's coat of arms were painted on the ceiling, possibly to encourage thoughts of England.

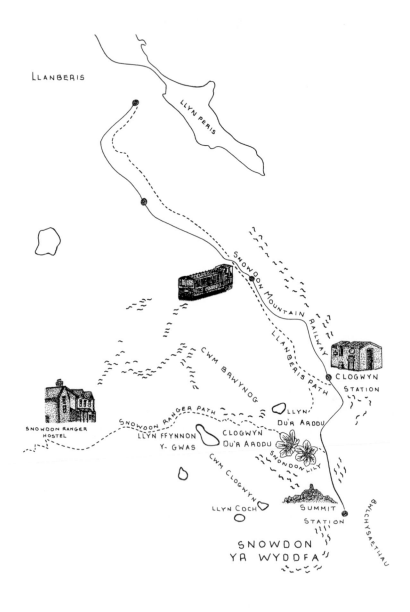

LLANBERIS

LLYN PERIS

SNOWDON MOUNTAIN RAILWAY

LLANBERIS PATH

CLOGWYN STATION

CWM BAWYNOG

SNOWDON RANGER PATH

SNOWDON RANGER HOSTEL

LLYN FFYNNON Y-GWAS

LLYN DU'R ARDDU

CLOGWYN DU'R ARDDU

SNOWDON LILY

CWM CLOGWYN

LLYN COCH

SUMMIT STATION

BWLCHYSAETHAU

SNOWDON
YR WYDDFA

5. SNOWDON

Hats in the air

The ascent of Snowdon, Yr Wyddfa, is always exciting. If you are in luck and there is little or no cloud the view from the top is magnificent: well worth panting for. From almost any angle the highest mountain in England and Wales has a splendid and magisterial pyramid appearance: it was created for artists.

As great mountains often are, it has for centuries been a storehouse of legends. It is well-known, for example, that King Arthur and his knights are slumbering under their duvets in a comfortable cave in Bwlchysaethau, the Pass of Arrows, awaiting the call to action; and it seems that every boulder has a tall or true tale attached to it.

I set off on the Snowdon Ranger Path, perhaps the oldest route to the top, a distance to the summit of about five miles. The Snowdon Ranger, now a youth hostel, used to be an inn. In the sixteenth century Snowdon formed part of the Royal Forest of Snowdon and the Earl of Leicester first held the office of Snowdon Ranger. I reckoned I should be able to reach the summit after three

Snowdon's challenge: Clogwyn Du'r Arddu

and a half hours' walking, taking another two hours or so to get down.

An attraction for tourists since the seventeenth century, Snowdon owed its first surge of real popularity to Napoleon Bonaparte. As the eighteenth century flowed into the nineteenth the wars with France made much of Europe out of bounds and put a temporary stop to the Grand Tours of young British gentlemen. They therefore sought other sensations.

Llyn Ffynnon-y-gwas

In Snowdonia they discovered an exotic alpine grandeur, a remote Celtic fastness exuding romance, a place for new experiences. They walked hard, dined hard and scribbled hard; and soon the bookshops were full of their lovingly-crafted accounts, drawings, verses and observations. To their minds, Snowdon was more than a climb. It was a melodrama, a journey to the awesome and forbidding abode of the gods, so that at almost every turn they indulged themselves in exclamation and ornate phrase – 'O terrible abyss!' George Borrow, who made the climb with his wife Henrietta, was so moved by the mountain's magnificence that he sang a Welsh verse at the top of his voice.

It soon became clear that it was not just the dramatic crags and inky pools the early male tourists admired. They were enchanted, too, by the delectable young women of Snowdonia.

'Pretty pouting lips,' wrote one.

'My Welsh beauty of Snowdon,' drooled another.

'The tendency to embonpoint, so characteristic of the Welch woman, was by no means displeasing in these young and elastic subjects,' gulped yet another.

These young fellows beheld a Snowdonian version of the noble savage and wrote lyrically of the girls' hair and eyes, their beautiful ankles, throbbing necks and the curve of their bosoms; so that one can only hope there was a cold bath at the end of a day of strenuous walking and imagining. No wonder, as it is recorded, that at least one farmer kept the prettier of his two daughters out of sight of these red-blooded English gentlemen.

But these same gents were a source of income to farmers and guides who lived on the slopes. Until the beginning of this century most visitors hired guides to conduct them to the summit. George Borrow met a guide who waggishly called himself the original Snowdon Ranger. These men were local personalities, sometimes celebrities. One of them, Robert Edwards, advertised himself as 'Guide-General and Magnificent Expounder of all the natural curiosities of North Wales; Professor of Grand and Bombastic lexicographical words; knight of the most anomalous, whimsical order of Hare-Brained Inexplicables.'

Guides would tout for business at Llanberis and Beddgelert stations. Lord Tennyson once hired a guide, but abandoned his ascent of the mountain because the weather was too cold. He went off for a walk by himself, returning to find the guide lying on his back and Lady Tennyson sitting on a chair, warming her bare feet on the man's chest ... 101 things to do with a Welshman.

Many visitors were interested in botany and geology and local people were happy to sell them crystals, fossils and plants. For a while in the nineteenth century there was a craze for ferns. The top guides knew where to find the rarest of them. William Williams, of the Victoria Hotel, Llanberis, who cut a romantic figure in his suit of goatskin, lowered himself down a cliff to harvest a shy fern and was killed when his rope broke. He was the most famous Snowdon guide of all – once advertised as 'the wild man of the mountain' – and his death was reported in *The Times* of London.

Eventually, as the major routes became established and guide books proliferated, visitors found they could climb the mountain without a guide and an extraordinary breed of men faded away. Some of them, goats in human form, would bound up and down the mountain two or three times in a day; and a few reached the summit five thousand times (or so they said).

After a steep climb, the valley slope became more gentle, and the tapestry unfolded. Not far off was Clogwyn y Gwin farm, once the home of 'the man who fired the last shot at the Battle of Waterloo'. The way he told it, he lay among the groaning wounded at the end of the day and watched a little old lady creeping among the injured men, hitting them on the head with a hammer before stealing their rings and other valuables. As she approached this son of Snowdon, he levelled his pistol and shot her dead.

Some hard work brought me the reward of Cwm Brwynog, a sublime panorama, and then the slope grew rough and stony, one of the most desolate stretches of the mountain, a pitiless terrain, the sort of landscape that made Victorian tourists shudder and caused ladies to grasp a fellow's arm and say: 'Oh, Albert, you're so strong.'

I was aware of the silence of a cathedral. In the middle of strewn rocky rubble, which had rolled like dice down the mountain, was the secret indigo pool, the Black Lake of Arddu. It was like a hard jewel guarded by the bulk of the Black Cliff, Clogwyn Du'r Arddu, a massive sentinel of rock talked about wherever climbing men

Beautiful and eerie: the Black Lake of Arddu

meet. It was here in 1800 that a Welsh parson and an English visitor made the first rock climb, the parson taking off his belt to help haul his friend to 'the brow of that dreadful precipice'. And here, in the 1950s, the remarkable and daring Joe Brown, in his early twenties and newly demobbed from the Services, made history and his reputation with his pioneering, revolutionary climbs.

At the end of the Black Lake, in the heart of this unforgiving place, I could see the remains of a copper mine, at two thousand feet the highest such mine in Britain. Only the toughest of the tough could work up here. The immense scars in the cliffs show where miners dug out the copper.

Shy beauty: the Snowdon lily

Not far off, I saw a figure abseiling as daintily as a spider down a cliff. Barbara Jones, a botanist, had a special licence to hunt for the shy and hardy Snowdon lily, one of the rarest flowers in Britain. It grows only on this small patch of cliff and flowers only for two weeks in a year. A few people in the know make a pilgrimage to see it. I felt privileged to see this little flower, the size of a sixpence with pale yellow petals, which, perversely, prefers to bloom among harsh rocks, battered by gales and concealed by chilly mists.

The path threaded past Clogwyn Coch. The huge rocks impose themselves upon you. They demand respect.

As I toiled up the track I met a young man and woman, descending. The man was wearing a dinner jacket and bow tie. Why, I asked, not minding my own business. 'Well,' he said, 'we met on Snowdon a year ago and started going out together. Eventually we decided that we would like to marry on the summit. Of course, there has to be an official ceremony, but we've just been on the top making our vows and that, we feel, is our true wedding.' And away they walked, smiling, arm in arm.

Visitor at Clogwyn station

On the ridge a steam engine of the Snowdon railway hauled itself upwards, trailing a streamer of smoke. The track was laid in 1896 amid protests that the pristine beauty of the mountain was being violated and complaints that it would be used by 'vulgar bun-and-whisky tourists'.

'Why should Snowdon be reserved for climbers?' retorted a railway company director. 'Are there not thousands who would like to inhale the exhilarating air and look down on the glorious panorama?'

Today, no doubt, the environmentalists would win the argument; but those were imperial days, the great age of the unstoppable all-conquering railway, and public opinion was strongly in favour. Purists prefer to walk, but the railway, and the cafe at the top are as much a part of the scene as the climbers. The original Swiss steam locomotives are the favourites. They haul themselves hand over hand up the mountain, a cog wheel gripping a toothed central track.

The five miles of railway were laid in a remarkable seventy-two working days. Eighty passengers bought tickets for the inaugural trip on Easter Monday 1896 and within the hour were at the top. Not long after this triumphant moment, a walker enjoying the tranquillity of the mountain was astonished to see a steam engine flying through the air above his head. The locomotive *Ladas* had lost its grip on the toothed track. The driver and fireman leapt to safety. Then, as now, locomotives were not coupled to the carriages and the quick-thinking railway manager applied the carriage brake and stopped safely. But a Llanberis hotelier panicked, jumped out and later died of his injuries. The following year a safety device was invented to prevent the trains jumping the track and there has been no serious incident since.

The cry 'Hang on to your hats' often came too late for train passengers in the open carriages on this windy ridge. So many

A Snowdon institution

caps, bonnets, boaters and bowlers blew into the valley below that it became known as Cwm Hetiau, Hat Valley.

Cloud was swirling around the summit, but visibility was good as I paced steadily upwards. I stopped at a small spring on my left. In Victorian times it was a popular halt for walking parties, though some always liked a stronger drink. One regular walker recorded: 'On the advice of the clergyman who attended me in this and other mountain excursions, I always took with us a pint of brandy, of which we used to drink without experiencing the slightest degree of intoxication.'

Traditionally, one of the favourite Snowdon experiences was to climb to the top to see the sunrise. Years ago, people boasted of the wonderful views, saying they could see all the way to Ireland and the Isle of Man, to Cumbria and even Scotland. Such clarity seems rarer today, perhaps because of air pollution. Still, I had a view of the triple peaks of Yr Eifl, 'the Rivals', twenty miles away down the Lleyn Peninsula.

More than 125,000 people take the train to the top every year. Still, most people walk up (Henry Thackwell was ninety when he did so in 1978) and some crazy men run up. These days you see hang gliders swooping around. In the last century a man tried to balloon to the top but missed the summit and landed in the Menai Strait.

A walk-on part in the Snowdon drama

Because it's there...

When I was only a few strides from the top, the view was suddenly blotted out by cloud. Capricious Snowdon was cheating me of my reward. I was reminded of a Victorian couple who laboured to the 3,560ft summit and huffily noted in the visitors' book that they could see nothing except the absurdity of their expedition.

The fact is that the summit is more often cloaked in cloud than not. The visibility was worsening by the second. There were only glimpses of lakes and distant mountains as the mist fell like a veil. As I stood on the top the wind suddenly blew hard. When the summit cafe was built sixty or so years ago its windows were smashed by the wind and had to be made smaller. The hotels built up here for Victorian tourists were lashed down by ropes secured to iron rings that can still be seen. These lodgings were Spartan places and one was known as the Cold Club.

The summit cafe is an ugly grey building, built for the extreme conditions, but I was grateful for the tea and the shelter as a squall raged. You can't expect to be on your own on Snowdon. The world and his wife come here. It's like the Eiffel Tower, irresistible. The people buy their summit tee-shirts and spend five pence to cover the cost of water that has to be hauled up by train so that it can be flushed down. Snowdonian solitude can easily be found elsewhere, away from the honeypot of Snowdon itself; and, in any case, there is an enduring pleasure in gazing at the mountain from a distance.

I headed down the path. The weather improved. The sun shone. It was a lovely evening in Llanberis.

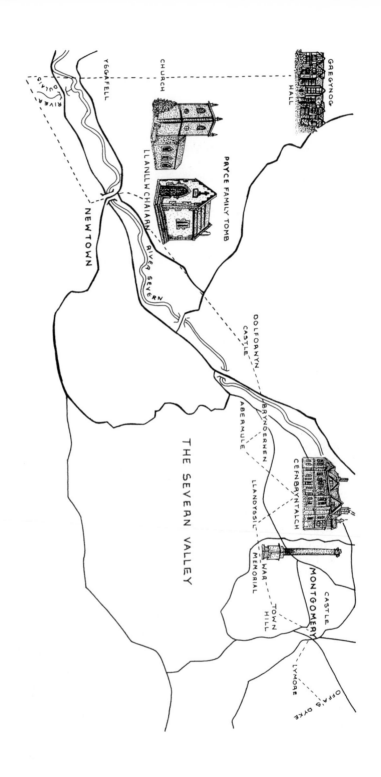

6. THE SEVERN VALLEY

The land of frozen ink

I started on the very edge of Wales, with the early morning sun on my back, at Offa's Dyke. Here Wales and England meet in an intricate and interlocking jigsaw. The border snakes around the line of the dyke, so that it seems that one step puts you in England and the next takes you into Wales: the Offa's Dyke tango.

Much of the earthwork was built on the orders of King Offa of Mercia in the eighth century. It is one of the most remarkable structures ever built in Britain. Thousands of labourers were recruited to work on it and it stretches from Chepstow to Prestatyn, though not in an unbroken line.

But it was never meant to be a frontier defended by soldiers, like Hadrian's Wall. No military forces were ever stationed on it. Offa's intention was to define the boundary of his own large kingdom of Mercia, to say to his Welsh neighbours: 'This is ours and that is yours'; and the line in many parts was fixed in consultation with local Welsh princes.

In the centuries that followed its construction, the dyke no

Jigsaw country

doubt helped to give the Welsh a sense of themselves and their geography. The modern shape of Wales, however, was not legally defined until the Acts of Union passed in Henry VIII's reign; and these also gave Wales equality with England.

I walked through Lymore Park with the castle-knobbed hill of Montgomery firmly in my sights. The hill's strategic location is the reason for the town's existence. It commands what was an important ford across the Severn, the road into Powys, and so its early history is a chronicle of fighting and frontier tensions. The town's Welsh name is Trefaldwyn. Its English name is actually French: from Roger of Montgomery, a Norman conqueror appointed as a Marcher Lord to bring this unruly part of Wales under control.

Montgomery is one of the delightful small towns of mid-Wales, as comfortable as an old tweed jacket, with a large square and fine Elizabethan and Georgian houses built onto a medieval street pattern. It looks a little like a town stolen from England and hauled across the border. Its people evidently enjoy a proper pride in its history and handsome appearance. I had a chat with Brian and Margery Richards who have made of Montgomery's mayoralty something of a Mom-and-Pop store: between them they have been mayor eleven times.

Through the cornfields into mid-Wales

The old school log book is displayed in the town museum, the teachers recording such events as 'Today the ink froze in the ink-well', 'I had to punish Charlie Jones for pinching Amy Sloan while trying to stuff de-worming powder down her throat', and 'I thrashed the stupidity out of J. Evans'. As we all know, schooldays are the happiest days of our lives.

The principal attractions of the thirteenth-century church are the rood screen and the marvellous tomb of Sir Richard Herbert, who died in 1596. Effigies of Sir Richard and his rosy-cheeked wife lie under an exquisitely-painted canopy, and behind are the kneel-ing figures of their eight children, looking as good as gold. The whole work, decorated with scrolls and pictures, is a celebratory sepulchre as gorgeous as a set of playing cards. At the feet of the Herberts lie two effigies, one of Sir Richard's grandfather and the second, almost certainly, of Edmund Mortimer, Owain Glyndwr's son-in-law.

In the churchyard I saw the grave of an obviously well-liked village policeman, with a helmet, lantern and truncheon carved into the stone. And I visited, as one must, the burial place of John Newton Davies, hanged for highway robbery in 1821. On the gallows outside the town jail he declared his innocence, saying that

Extravagant, exquisite: the tomb of the Herberts

as proof of it no grass would grow on his grave for a hundred years. Many witnesses testified that the grave did indeed remain barren, but perhaps so many tourists came, with their big boots, that grass never had a chance to grow. There is some grass today, but also a lot of bald patches.

Broken sword: Montgomery Castle

I walked out of the town to the rocky ridge on which the castle ruins rise, well worth the effort because the views of the quilted hills beyond the flowery cottage gardens are wonderful. The castle was built here by Henry III in 1223. Four centuries later, during the Civil War, it was given up to Parliamentary troops and much of it was subsequently demolished.

Ivor Tanner, an enthusiastic and engaging Montgomery stone-mason, who used to work for Cadw, the Welsh heritage body, bubbled with enthusiasm as he gave me an account of his amazing excavation of the castle well. It was found in 1966, under the rubble left by the demolition of 1649, and was full of stones. Ivor and his men started to dig out this rubble and when they reached fifty-five feet they began bailing water with a ten-gallon milk churn. The work went on for years and for some of the time the intrepid Ivor excavated alone, descending by a series of ladders. An electric water pump made the work easier. In 1974, Ivor reached his deepest point, at two hundred feet. He found a pistol holster, a silver candlestick and the wooden barrel that, centuries before, had been used to haul up the water. It wasn't the bottom of the well – more rubble lay beneath – but Ivor, the human mole, was ordered by his bosses to call it a day, although he wanted to go on.

Stone of remembrance: the county war memorial

From the castle I made my way to the top of Town Hill. The county war memorial obelisk was placed here because it can be seen from most of the county. The naked trees nearby reminded me of those in sepia photographs of First World War battlefields, stripped and shattered by shellfire. They and the memorial lend a poignancy to the view. Looking out over the landscape I could understand what is meant when people talk of 'mwynder Maldwyn,' the gently rumpled velvet softness of Montgomeryshire and its enfolded little towns.

I made my way through meadows and lanes into Llandyssil and walked on to little Abermule in the Severn valley. To my right stood Cefnbryntalch, the home for some years of Philip Heseltine, the composer, who used the pseudonym Peter Warlock. Born in 1894, he lived a bohemian life in London and took the name of Warlock while under the influence of Aleister Crowley, the sinister occultist who styled himself The Great Beast. He moved to Bryntalch, escaping Crowley's black magic, and submitted to his

Cefnbryntalch: haven for a tortured soul

mother's strict but beneficial regime. He went for long walks in the Welsh hills and during this time, the most creative of his life, wrote his finest music. The demon he never defeated was alcohol. His life ended at thirty-six in a gas-filled room in London; but whether his death was an accident, suicide or, as has been suggested, murder, was never clear.

In Abermule I watched pupils at the school performing a drama based on the train crash of 1921, a head-on collision in which seventeen people were killed, including Lord Herbert Vane-Tempest, a director of the Cambrian Railway. Some of his wealth was inherited by his kinsman, Winston Churchill, who, in those days, was very hard up. It was a most fortunate windfall, bringing stability to the Churchill finances.

I crossed the river by Brynderwen Bridge and climbed the steep path to the evocative ruins of Dolforwyn Castle. Here history turned. This was the last fortress built by a Welsh prince. Llywelyn ordered it to be built in 1273, when he was at the height of his powers: the Treaty of Montgomery in 1267 had recognised him as Prince of Wales.

Edward I was mightily affronted when he heard of the castle's construction, seeing it as the threatening nucleus of a new Welsh capital. He ordered Llywelyn to pull it down. No, said Llywelyn. In 1277, in response to this defiance, Edward sent an army across the Severn from Montgomery. Dolforwyn castle fell ignominiously in nine days because its defenders had no water. For Llywelyn this reverse was the beginning of the end. The war with Edward ended with Llywelyn's death in 1282.

Llanllwchaiarn Church

I walked the valley to Llanllwchaiarn church and admired its rare and lovely pre-Raphaelite stained glass windows by William Morris, Sir Edward Burne-Jones and Ford Madox Brown. A few minutes more and I was in bustling Newtown which was new a long time ago: it was chartered in the thirteenth century. Since the 1960s it has been an expanding commercial centre with a role in bringing life to mid-Wales and stemming depopulation.

In the old churchyard I inspected the tomb of the Pryce family. Of Sir John Pryce, born 1698, it can be said that he certainly loved his wives. When the first one died he had her embalmed and placed beside his bed. When the second Lady Pryce died he had her embalmed, too, and put on the other side. One version of the story has it that the wives were actually in his bed. However, his third wife, who married him in 1741, drew the line at sharing the

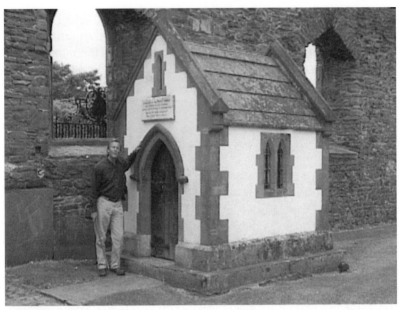

The tomb of Sir John Pryce, who could not say goodbye

bedroom with her two stuffed predecessors and demanded that they be buried. Sir John reluctantly agreed that when it comes to wives in the bedroom, three is a crowd.

Just outside the churchyard is the memorial to Newtown's most famous old boy, Robert Owen, the Utopian socialist and factory reformer. He left the town when he was ten and did not return until 1858 when he was eighty-seven. He announced: 'I will lay down my bones whence I derived them', booked into the Bear Hotel and, not long after, died there.

In his boyhood Robert Owen knew the clattering looms, bustle and hard labour of the woollen mills where some of the workers

Memorial to Robert Owen

were children as young as seven. Newtown was the Welsh capital of flannel manufacture, with abundant supplies of wool and plenty of water to drive the mill wheels. It had an imposing Flannel Exchange – and flannel is one of the few Welsh words that has passed into English. The wool came down from the hills and Newtown set to work: it oiled it, willowed it, scribbled it, carded it, slubbed it, spun it, wound it, warped it, sized it and wove it on more than a thousand looms.

A later hero of Newtown was Sir Pryce Pryce-Jones, the inventor of mail order and parcel post, whose name stands high above the town on the roof of his magnificent red brick Royal Welsh Warehouse.

By Appointment

Pryce-Jones was a go-getter. He displayed Welsh flannel at exhibitions throughout the world and conceived the idea of distributing catalogues to prospective clients. One of his big customers was Florence Nightingale; and another was Queen Victoria. A large order from Windsor Castle in 1869 set the church bells in Newtown ringing in celebration; and a portrait of the Queen is incorporated in the main stained glass window of the parish church. Orders for flannel came in from other royal houses in Europe; and Pryce-Jones supplied flannel blankets to the Russian and Prussian armies. One of his inventions was the sleeping bag.

The first mail order parcels went from Newtown by stage coach, and later by special rail carriages to London. Sir John's idea of a parcel post was taken up by the Post Office.

The benefactress of Newtown, in stained glass

The path out of the town took me past the Dolerw estate and into the hills. Across the valley lies Ysgafell Farm where something remarkable happened in the seventeenth century. The farmer was a strict Puritan, persecuted for his dissident religious beliefs. He was thrown into jail, his farm was burnt, his animals were taken and it seemed certain his family would starve. But a late crop of wheat produced an astonishingly abundant harvest, a lifesaver, and the field is still known as Cae'r Fendith, the field of the blessing.

Near here in June 1936 Bernice Roberts had the adventure and moment of glory which remains vivid in her memory. In graphic detail, she told me all about it.

The River Dulais had been swollen by heavy rain and threatened the railway bridge over the river. Bernice went out with her father, a retired railwayman, and as the storm raged and trees were washed like matchsticks down the river, they saw the bridge collapse. They knew a train would be along soon. Bernice ran as fast as she could to the signal box at Newtown station to raise the alarm. It was a desperate two-mile run. The train was stopped just in time. Bernice showed me the treasured memento of 'the day I'll never forget' – a copy of the *Daily Express* with the front page headline Woman Races Through Storm To Save Excursion Train.

Heading northwards, I came to the remains of the old lead mine at Melin-y-gloch. It was known, with good reason, as a swindle mine. In the 1870s a mine not far from here was the most profitable lead producer in the country and the Melin-y-gloch mine was excavated in the hope that it would do just as well. It did not; but the miners encouraged Lord Joicey, a Northumberland coal owner, to invest money in the enterprise. They employed a simple deception. They bought lead ore from another mine and took it to their own, where they showed it to Lord Joicey to lever more cash from him.

Joicey, incidentally, was briefly owner of Gregynog Hall, near Tregynon, which stands in splendour amidst woods and parkland. From the mid-fifteenth century it was the seat of the Blayney family and was famous for its generous table and hospitality to visiting bards: not a bad reputation. In the nineteenth century the house was rebuilt and enclosed in a concrete shell, painted to look

Gregynog Hall

Gregynog Hall enigma

like a timber-framed Elizabethan mansion. The Hanbury-Tracy family who owned it were pioneers in the use of concrete and several houses in the neighbourhood were built of this material.

The woodland around Gregynog is rated a Site of Special Scientific Interest. The aptly-named Ray Woods, a lichen special-ist, told me that more than 130 species of lichen grow here. 'Gregynog is to my mind the equivalent of a temperate rain forest, where all sorts of mosses and lichens thrive. There is an abundance of mature and veteran trees and I see them as tower blocks of rich wildlife, supporting fungi, beetles and rare lichens.

'One of the lichens here is of the kind that used to be mixed with urine and fermented to produce a red colour used in the dyeing of kilts in Scotland. There are also two species of the rare tree lungwort used to make a purple dye. Now there's only just enough of that lichen in mid-Wales to dye a bobble hat.'

Gregynog had a famous flowering when it was bought in the 1920s by the sisters Gwendoline and Margaret Davies, grand-daughters of David Davies of Llandinam, the larger-than-life Victorian engineer and coal entrepreneur. They transformed the house into a centre for music and art. The leading musicians and orchestras made their way to Gregynog. The staff choir was

Gardens at Gregynog

renowned. I like the teasing tale that advertisements used to say: Gardeners Wanted For Gregynog – Only Tenors Need Apply. The house was also famous for exquisite printing, the Gregynog Press being an outstanding private press; and, meanwhile, the Davies sisters accumulated one of the great collections of Impressionist paintings, now in the National Museum. Gregynog is now part of the University of Wales.

The most interesting part of the house is the Blayney Room of 1636, with its rich and intricate panelling, displaying the coats of arms of the old princes and noble families of Wales. It is a boast room, really. As Dr Glyn Tegai Hughes, a former Warden of Gregynog remarked, the coats of arms are of 'families to whom the Blayneys were related, or to whom they wished it to be thought that they were related'.

Great families, like empires, rise and fall. When Arthur Blayney, last of the Blayneys of Gregynog, died in 1795 he insisted on a quiet exit, no funeral service, no crowds, a simple country hearse, and a burial so early in the morning that no crowd would gather to gawp. 'The better sort, I presume, will not intrude as there is no invitation.'

Thus he tiptoed out of life. It seemed just the right place to finish my walk and set off for a bath and dinner.

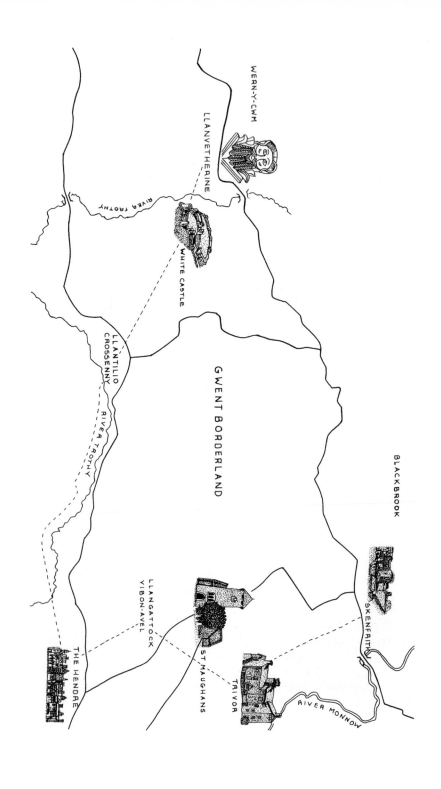

WERN-Y-CWM

LLANVETHERINE

RIVER TROTHY

WHITE CASTLE

LLANTILIO
CROSSENNY

RIVER TROTHY

GWENT BORDERLAND

BLACKBROOK

LLANGATTOCK
VIBON-AVEL

THE HENDRE

ST MAUGHANS

TRIVOR

SKENFAITH

RIVER MONNOW

7. GWENT BORDERLAND

Duw, those boys did well

Frontiers are always exciting. For me they promise adventure. In many places, borderlands form a kind of third country, where neighbouring languages, traditions and points of view slop and overflow into one another, sometimes happily, sometimes uneasily.

The border country of Wales is not only a rich repository of history and fable; it is also lovely to look at and ideal for walking. I chose a reasonably demanding journey of sixteen miles from Llanvetherine to Skenfrith through typical border landscape, hilly, fertile and lovely, the plough revealing soil as red as liver. It is well-castled, too, the enduring evidence of the warfare and political tensions centuries ago. Allow your imagination to get the better of you and you'll fancy you can hear the clash of swords and the terrible hiss of arrows.

The church in Llanvetherine, my starting point, has two remarkable life-sized stone effigies which show clearly, like an illustration in a newspaper fashion page, what well-dressed men and women wore in Stuart times. Judging by his effigy, the Reverend David Powell, who died in 1621 and was vicar of Llanvetherine for

Llanvetherine

The well-dressed parson and his wife

forty-three years, was something of a dandy. Here he is in his knee breeches, a knotted belt and a cloak embroidered with oak leaves. His beard is plaited in what today we would call Rastafarian style; and his moustache is just made for twirling.

On the other side of the altar is his dear wife, with plump cheeks and her Sunday-best tall hat, her hands clasped in prayer. Her wedding ring is on the second finger of her right hand, although it was decreed in 1549 that such rings should be worn on the left hand. So she was stubbornly traditional. She wears an expensive embroidered skirt. Her feet in their smart little shoes have been carved at right angles, and they look rather odd, but that was the artistic convention of the time.

In many villages the local blacksmith, well used to repairing carts and carriages, became a mechanic when the motor car arrived on the scene. Certainly the garage in Llanvetherine used to be the smithy. Cyril Lane, the owner, told me that his grandfather, William Dable Lane, was the champion blacksmith of the British Empire, a title he won in competitions. His skills earned him the Freedom of the City of London and brought him to the notice of King Edward VII.

'The King wanted him to join his staff as chief farrier, but grandfather was a stubborn man and said he would work for himself and no-one else. So a system was devised. The king sent his horses by rail to Abergavenny and grooms brought them up here to the smithy to be shod. When the job was done the horses were out on the train back to London.'

You can imagine how proud the villagers must have been to see all the King's horses coming to their village.

From the path, as I made my way east along the edge of a hillside meadow, I had a view of Wern-y-Cwm, once the home of Captain Thomas James, a pioneer Arctic explorer and evidently as tough as teak. In 1631-32 he led an expedition, financed by Bristol merchants, in search of the North West Passage linking the Arctic to the Pacific. In honour of his native land he gave the name of South Wales to a peninsula. It was a bleak and icy place: perhaps he was indulging his sense of humour. His vivid descriptions of the bitter Arctic winter inspired Coleridge to write *The Rime of the Ancient Mariner.*

White Castle: splendid isolation

One of the key points of my walk, a few miles from Llanvetherine, was White Castle, Castell Gwyn, isolated and commanding on its hill. Castles like this remind us that conquest was a slow and frequently brutal business and that castles, as well as being defences, were a show of force, mailed fists cracking down on restless people. The stonework of the castle was painted and plastered white, which would have enhanced its appearance, at once majestic and awesome. It remains in magnificent condition because there is no settlement nearby. Many castles are ruins because they were regarded as quarries, a source of good quality stone, and their stones were carted away to build houses.

A fort was built here in Norman times, but the castle in its present form, like so many in Wales, dates from the twelfth and thirteenth centuries, the period of gradual English conquest, border wars and the Marcher Lords who controlled the Marches, the borderlands. The countryside around here was aflame during the rebellion against English rule led by Owain Glyndwr in the first years of the fifteenth century. He raided many places in this region, wrecked Tretower, sacked Abergavenny and Newport, burnt Hay, took Cardiff and besieged Grosmont.

The arrow loops set in the walls of White Castle are unusually deep and narrow. Peter Jones, an historian, provided me with an

White Castle: arrow routes

explanation. First he reminded me of the deadly skills of Welsh archers in the middle ages. With their rough, short, elmwood bows they could send an arrow through a timber door four fingers thick. Their marksmanship was so good that, standing outside a castle, they could shoot an arrow into the narrow fissure of an arrow loop and kill a man standing there. A bowman inside the castle would stand well back from the loop because he knew that an arrow formed an S-shape when it left the bow, so he made allowance for it to snake through the loop on its way to the target. The arrow loops at White Castle have unique horizontal slits which, Peter Jones thought, were a device to help defenders sight their targets.

In 1942 the castle was visited several times by that strange prisoner of war, Rudolf Hess, Hitler's deputy. He had parachuted into Scotland in 1941 and after a spell in the Tower of London was transferred to a clinic at Maindy Court, near Abergavenny, and kept under heavy guard. At the castle, his minders allowed him to wander the battlements and look over the mountains. Sometimes he would make sketches. He would never know such freedom again. The Nuremberg trials lay ahead ... and lifelong imprisonment in Spandau.

One of his guards in Wales was Joe Clifford, who met me at the castle to talk about him. 'Visiting local beauty spots was part of his treatment and he particularly liked the castle. He was very aloof and distant, and hardly ever spoke, a proud man. He used to walk in a semi-goosestep, and still thought of himself as the deputy Führer.'

It is one of the curiosities of history that Hess's father, Carl, once worked in south Wales and married a woman from Michaelston-y-fedw, near Cardiff. She died in Germany and her body was brought back for burial in Michaelston. Carl married again – and the son of this marriage was Rudolf Hess.

Hen Gwrt: a long way from Agincourt

About a mile from the castle, as I followed the Offa's Dyke Path, I came to the traces of Hen Gwrt, the Old Court. It is just a moated island today, but there is a local belief, which some dispute, that it was the home of Sir Dafydd Gam who was possibly the model for Shakespeare's brave and fiery Welshman Fluellen (though the Elizabethan soldier Sir Roger Williams is a likelier candidate). Shakespeare teased the Welsh a little in his plays, but he was usually nice about them. It's said that he had a Welsh grandmother.

We do not know much about Dafydd Gam except that he was killed fighting at Agincourt in 1415. He is credited in stories with saving the life of Henry V on the battlefield and telling the King before the battle that there were 'enough French to be killed, enough to be taken prisoner and enough to run away.'

Legend says that if all the sons and daughters of this robust man had linked hands they would have formed a chain a quarter of a mile long. His coat of arms, showing three heads with the necks in the slithery coils of serpents, can be seen both at the pub and the church at Llantilio Crossenny.

On a pillar in the church is the carved head of a 'green man',

Green Man at Llantilio Crossenny

with grotesquely lolling tongue and curling hair, a fertility symbol in pre-Christian times. The church did not despise such pagan devices. It incorporated them into the Christian faith.

The path from Llantilio Crossenny swoops south, not far from Offa's Dyke. I walked through the valley of the River Trothy, as tentative sunshine shone through the clouds and dappled the hills, and came to a place dedicated to the bottling of sunlight. Here in his vineyard the resilient Peter Johnson struggles with nature and works at producing, among other wines, a Welsh claret. If you choose to grow grapes in Wales you are bound to be something of a fighter and a gambler. As Peter told me over a glass of his dry white, he knows the crop will be ruined by frost one year in five.

My route now took me to the Hendre estate, once one of the grandest in Gwent, the six-thousand acre home of the Rolls family, who made their wealth originally out of property in London.

The brilliant son of the house, heir to Lord Llangattock, was Charlie Rolls, whose name was allied, in 1904, with that of the engineer Henry Royce. Charlie Rolls was a pioneer motorist and in London in 1899 was fined for breaking the 4 m.p.h. speed limit and failing to employ a man with a red flag to walk in front of him. He was also a balloonist and one of the earliest British aviators. He bought an aircraft from the Wright brothers and was the first man to make a return flight across the Channel. There is a good statue of him in the square in Monmouth.

The Hendre: fancies of flight

In the end, his passion for flying cost him his life. His plane crashed in front of a horrified crowd at an air show in Bournemouth in 1910 and he died on the grass surrounded by his friends. He was the first Briton killed in a flying accident. I visited his grave in Llangattock churchyard and reflected that he had once, in his lighthearted way, talked of 'entering the golden gates on wings.'

The Hendre estate has been broken up now and men play golf where Charlie Rolls wrestled with the challenges of flight. Before the Second World War the estate was a semi-feudal society, a rural kingdom, and all the workers lived in a model village built and owned by the estate. The shepherds, the foresters, the gamekeepers, the bailiffs, the waggoners, gardeners, smiths and cowgirls all had their fine houses, some of which were adorned with the Rolls motto Celeritas et Veritas: speed and truth. The same inscription adorns Charlie Rolls's gravestone. The estate houses are now

Estate workers' houses

privately owned. The former smithy remains a place of craftsmanship, albeit rather quieter. In place of hammer and anvil there is the pen and ink of Donald Jackson, who heads a group of calligraphers working with traditional goose quills to produce beautiful manuscripts. There is a good demand for this work, in testimonials, civic documents and awards, a gratifying preference for hand skills in our computer age.

The skills are a link with the monks and clerks who painstak-ingly copied and illuminated the great books and manuscripts in the centuries before the printing press. I asked Donald what happened when he, literally, made a slip of the pen. 'I say much he same thing as the old monks,' he laughed, 'only they said it in Latin.'

St Maughans: exotic link

My next stop was the pretty church of St Maughans. It was restored by Charles Rolls's grandfather when it was fashionable for country gentlemen to show their piety by paying for church modernisation. On a plaque inside I found the exotic coat of arms of the King of Kandy in Ceylon, now Sri Lanka. Sir Robert Brownrigg, who is buried here, defeated the King and acquired Ceylon for the British Empire, and as a reward was allowed to attach the Kandy arms to his own. Incidentally, an old literary name for Ceylon was Serendib, from which we get the word serendipity, making happy discoveries by accident. That, needless to say, is a part of any walk in Wales.

I stopped at the handsome house called Trivor and was shown its secrets by the owner, Iorwerth Harries, who is restoring it. In the 1670s, anti-Catholic feelings, often amounting to hysteria, ran

Trivor: the secret room

very high after the conspirator Titus Oates invented the Popish Plot, supposedly a Catholic plan to kill King Charles II. Catholics were hounded and forced to worship in secret.

The valley in which Trivor lies was a stronghold of Catholicism and the house itself was the hiding place of a priest, Father John Lloyd, of Brecon. Iorwerth took me up the old, creaking stairs to the top of the house and showed me where the priest conducted services for the family. The hooks on which an altar cloth was hung are still there; and, among the beams, is a small chamber, a hide-out. In spite of the secrecy and precautions, Father Lloyd was eventually arrested at Trivor in 1678 and taken to Cardiff Castle where, the following year, he was hanged, drawn and quartered. He and Philip Evans, another priest executed at the same time, were canonized in 1970.

The footpath to Skenfrith beckoned me through a large planta-tion of poplars. The afternoon light and the shivering of the leaves created an ethereal atmosphere, as if I were finding my way through a mystical maze. I reached the River Monnow, with England on the other side, just a crossbow shot away, and tramped up to the ridge overlooking Skenfrith. The village was so peaceful and quiet I supposed that everyone was enjoying a siesta.

I walked down to visit the small castle. It was one of the trio of fortifications, along with White Castle and Grosmont, built by the

Skenfrith Castle with St Bridget's Church: treasures

Marcher Lord Hubert de Burgh to secure a grip on the Welsh border. The walls in Skenfrith were long ago robbed of stones to build houses in the neighbourhood.

Close by is the lovely church of St Bridget, with its dainty dovecote tower, and inside hangs the treasure of Skenfrith, an early sixteenth-century cope richly decorated with gold thread, double-headed eagles, pomegranates and figures of angels. It was discovered, doing duty as a communion table cloth, in the mid-nineteenth century. Kirstie Buckland, who restored it in three years of painstaking work, and told me its story, remarked that it would have been very dangerous to own such a thing during the years when Catholics were hounded.

The cope may have been hidden at Blackbrook, a house nearby, which was once the home of Sir Richard Morgan. He famously presided over the trial of Lady Jane Grey, who reigned as Queen of England for nine days. He sentenced her to death. The trial was rigged, of course, and Sir Richard was driven mad by remorse.

His brother John was the last Governor of Skenfrith Castle, and his tomb in the church testifies that he was an Elizabethan gentleman of substance. The carvings on the side of the tomb show the old man in a long gown and cap. His four sons are fine fellows swaggering in their doublets and hose. Floating above their shoulders are beaver hats, which in those days were an expensive status symbol.

You have to smile at the swank of it all. You can imagine the neighbours saying: 'Duw, look at those hats ... those Morgan boys have done well.'

Morgans: getting ahead with their hats

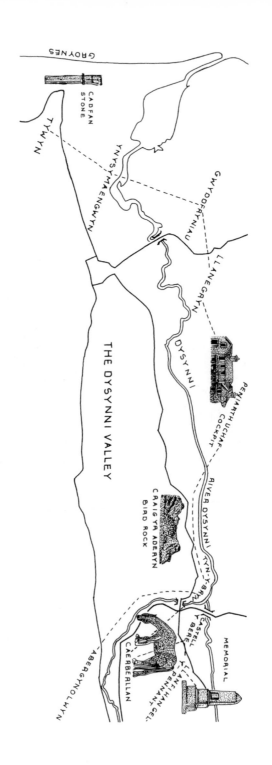

THE DYSYNNI VALLEY

GROYNES

CADFAN STONE

TYWYN

YNYS-Y-MAENGWYN

GWYDDFRYNIAU

LLANEGRYN

DYSYNNI

PENIARTH UCHAF
COCKPIT

RIVER DYSYNNI / TYN-Y-BRYN

CRAIG YR ADERYN
BIRD ROCK

CASTELL
Y BERE

MEMORIAL

CAERBERLLAN

CASTELL PENNANT
LLANFIHANGEL-Y-PENNANT

ABERGYNOLWYN

8. THE DYSYNNI VALLEY

Down the secret valley to the sea

It's a dozen miles or so from the old slate town of Abergynolwyn, my starting point, to Tywyn and the sea. I followed the course of the River Dysynni, which emerges from Tal-y-llyn lake. Its valley, one of the loveliest in Wales, has always been a rather secret place, never a well-trodden path. None of the early travellers and writers in Wales ventured this way. Thomas Pennant didn't, nor the indefatigable George Borrow; and few modern guide books pay it much attention, so there's a sense of exploring little-known country.

Out of Abergynolwyn the river takes a sharp and rather unexpected turn to the north and carves a narrow gorge, over a mile long, which is steep-sided, wild and rocky. It makes for a rewarding walk; and I did it on a sunny day under the watchful gaze of buzzards and hawks. After a while, the river seems to decide what it wants to do in life, turns south west and opens out into the valley proper.

At Ty'n-y-bryn I paused at the birthplace of William Owen

Buzzard-eye view: the Dysynni valley

Ty'n-y-bryn: the flawed lexicographer's home

Pughe, a considerable Welsh scholar and romantic, who adored Wales and the Welsh language. He wrote indifferent poetry and in 1803 famously published a Welsh-English dictionary of 100,000 words. He tried to demonstrate that Welsh was the language of heaven, that it had a common root with Hebrew. He cheated to reinforce his theories and filled the dictionary with words that didn't exist in Welsh. This muddied the literary waters for many years. On the other hand, Pughe's genuine scholarship helped to save much early Welsh writing.

He was erudite, kind-hearted and gullible. He published the wonderful fabrications of the great romancer Iolo Morgannwg, the inventor of the Gorsedd of Bards. Thus he was one of the actors in a colourful, creative and significant period in Welsh cultural life.

He was also a devotee of the prophetess and mystic Joanna Southcott and was one of those present at the autopsy performed on her in 1814. Her followers believed that she was pregnant with the Messiah and for this reason kept her body warm with hot water bottles for four days. Pughe wrote of the disappointment of her disciples when the post-mortem search revealed that her womb was empty.

In a meadow up the lane, at Caerberllan, I saw some of the finest shire horses in Britain, real champions. William Jones, the farmer who breeds them, showed me their finer points, the way

Equine beauties

they carry themselves, the way they hold their heads, the characteristics of superior horses. His champion mare Caerberllan Gold Gift comes from a line of winners: her mother, grandmother and great-grandmother were all champs.

Picking my way up the rocky grey slope of Castell y Bere, I felt rather like Tom Thumb scrambling up the tail of a mighty fallen dragon. In a sense, that is what it is.

At the summit of the outcrop I came to the ruins of the castle whose name is engraved on the Welsh imagination. Castell y Bere was built by Llywelyn the Great in 1221, with the distinctive D-shaped towers of Welsh-built fortifications, and was one of the strategically important castles in the age when Wales was ruled by princes. It was the last place of resistance to Edward I in his conquest of Wales in the thirteenth century and, after a siege of ten days, it was surrendered and destroyed. Dafydd, the brother of Llywelyn, the last native Prince of Wales, escaped from here but was captured and then hanged and dismembered at Shrewsbury. King Edward himself came to the castle in 1295. As I stood atop the ruins, I imagined him at this very place, looking out reflectively at the valley's grandeur, as if to satisfy himself that the dragon really was dead.

Mary Jones's memorial: famous footprints

A short distance up the valley I came to the hamlet of Llanfihangel-y-pennant, the setting of a very Victorian story of goodness and piety, the sort of thing adults told as a sermon to improve their children. A cottage here was the home of Mary Jones, a weaver's daughter, who, in 1800, when she was sixteen, walked across the mountains to Bala to buy a Welsh bible from the Reverend Thomas Charles.

Her story has been retold many times in books and pamphlets. Nearly two centuries on, it may be difficult for us to comprehend the impact it had in its day, but Mary's famous walk, twenty-five miles on bare feet (most country children went shoeless in those days), was a symbol of the wish of ordinary people for education and religious knowledge. She had saved three shillings and sixpence over six years to buy her bible. Thomas Charles had sold all his stock of bibles but was so impressed by Mary's devotion that he gave her his own; and Mary's example was an inspirational factor in the founding of the British and Foreign Bible Society.

I peeped into Peniel Methodist chapel, still used one Sunday a month by local farming families. I'm always fascinated by these small outposts of faith in remote places, some of them not much larger than sentry boxes. Often, as in this case, the harmonium tells the story of years of worship: its keys are well-worn and the instrument played its last hymn long ago.

Craig yr Aderyn: cormorants' kingdom

Craig yr Aderyn, the Bird Rock, imposes its handsome jutting profile on the flat-bottomed valley. As I walked towards it I caught its distinctive guano smell on the breeze. It is the only inland nesting place for cormorants in Britain. The sea used to wash against this steep seven-hundred foot cliff. Perhaps the birds have been too busy nesting and searching for food to notice that it has been thousands of years since the tide went out. Now they are six miles from the sea where they hunt for fish. Charles Darwin, the scientist, used to travel up here to shoot cormorants.

In the grounds of Peniarth Uchaf mansion, across the valley, there used to be a regular test of Darwin's ideas of the survival of the fittest, a cockpit. It is still there and you have to imagine the people crowded around this ring, raucous and colourful, cheering, shouting and making their bets, with hundreds of guineas changing hands as the birds tore themselves to pieces.

Until it was outlawed as a cruel spectacle in 1849, cockfighting was fashionable and immensely popular and played a large part in the life of rural Wales. Fights were often held on Sundays and announced in churches. They were well-patronised by magistrates, rectors and curates.

Betting shop: cockpit at Peniarth Uchaf

Peniarth Uchaf, by the way, is said to be the first house in Wales to serve a cup of tea. But the tale is told about other houses, too, and always has the same ending: that the people boiled up the tea, threw away the water and ate the hot mush of tea leaves with a spoon.

I had grand views as I walked down the valley, but I reflected that it was not always as peaceful as it looked. In the seventeenth century, particularly, highwaymen lurked on roads and bandits roamed the district, attacking and robbing farms. From time to time, local people joined in the raids to plunder their neighbours' property: community spirit was sometimes pretty thin.

The footpath took a turn through a gate and threaded through the rockeries and shrubs of a garden that was obviously lovingly tended. Jane Whittle, whose garden it was, took me to a barn nearby and showed me the work of art that she and her friends were painstakingly creating. It was a large tapestry of the whole Dysynni valley. Each woman was responsible for stitching a small section, an embroidered representation of a part of the valley she knew well. It had the look of a wonderful quilt. And when I set off again, down the valley, I had a sense of walking through the tapestry I had just seen. Incidentally, this lovely work can now be seen

Lap of the god: statue in Jane Whittle's garden

in the church at Llanfihangel-y-pennant.

On my right, concealed among the trees, stood noble Peniarth, a house which has been in the Wynne family since the fifteenth century. William Williams-Wynne, who kindly showed me around this lovely house, reminded me, with a rueful smile, that, years ago, when I was a reporter on *The Times*, I wrote an article about his attempt to win the parliamentary seat of Montgomery. The headline was Will William Williams-Wynne Win? (The answer, as it turned out, was No).

His ancestor, the historian and bibliophile William Watkin Edward Wynne, became the owner of the marvellous library collected at Hengwrt by Robert Vaughan, in the seventeenth century. It was the most important collection of Welsh manuscripts ever held in private hands and its priceless treasures included the Black Book of Carmarthen, which dates from about 1250, the Laws of Hywel Dda and the Book of Taliesin.

In 1898, this collection, known as the Peniarth Manuscripts, was bought by Sir John Williams, a physician to Queen Victoria (we encounter him again in the walk near Llansteffan in Carmarthenshire), and it became a founding jewel of the National Library in Aberystwyth.

Peniarth: priceless heritage

It was not far from Peniarth to Llanegryn, the star attraction of which is the rood screen in the church. There is a story that it was originally in Cymer Abbey at Dolgellau and that, at the time when Henry VIII dissolved the monasteries, the monks there, fearing it would be looted or wrecked, hauled it over the mountain and hid it here. Some say it was floated around on a raft, by river and sea. More likely, it is the loving work of a local craftsman. A proud note in a pamphlet in the church says 'This rood loft and its screen is probably the most famous in the world.'

Llanegryn was once a thriving place, noted for its learning and love of debate. A school was founded here in 1659 to teach Latin and Greek to the sons of the gentry. Prince Louis Lucien Bonaparte came here in 1855 in search of volumes to add to his collection of Celtic books and was amazed to find that so many people in the village had libraries.

As I headed towards Tywyn, the panorama of the mountains clear against the vivid blue sky reminded me of a long walk I once made in western Patagonia,

Rood screen, Llanegryn

in the district the first Welsh settlers there called Cwm Hyfryd, the 'lovely valley'.

I came to the ruins of a house at Gwyddfryniau which has one of the better ghost stories attached to it – and Wales has many of them. The house was haunted by the ghost of a housemaid. Every night, her screeching and wailing drove the terrified family into the fields. A schoolmaster came to challenge the ghost and bravely sat by the light of a candle, reading his bible. Just before midnight he smelt a foul odour and heard the blood-chilling screeching of the ghost. He fled, clutching his bible. Then the vicar came to exorcise the house. He fought an epic battle with the ghost – he recalled that there was the terrible smell of Satan in the air – but in the end he trapped the housemaid's spirit in a bottle and laid it to rest in the waters of the Dysynni, under a bridge.

Gwyddfryniau: the exorcist

I passed a farm which stands on the site of a manor, where, in medieval times, princes of the House of Gwynedd would come to collect their taxes. They accepted the taxes in the form of food and would promptly eat the lot.

The smell of the sea was quite strong now. As I always do in the last stages of a walk, I quickened my step. An obstacle lay ahead. Ten miles back the river was a narrow stream and I could have jumped across it. Now it had matured and broadened. My map showed a right of way across it and I suppose I could have swum to the opposite bank. Prudently, I had arranged for a small boat to be waiting and I rowed across in solemn dignity, stepping ashore dryshod. But you can just as easily cross by the bridge and walk into Bryncrug.

Ynysymaengwyn: a banished wife

The final furlongs crossed what used to be the estate of the grand mansion of Ynysymaengwyn. The house has gone now, having been used for fire brigade practice, but some of the estate's magnificent trees survive. If they could speak they would tell us about the former master of Ynysymaengwyn, John Corbett, the MP for Droitwich in the 1870s. He dreamed of transforming Tywyn into a swanky resort and built its promenade, leaving his name on several granite and marble plaques in the town.

Painfully aware that his name was spelt with two Ts, he dearly wanted to find a connection with the old aristocratic family of Corbet, spelt with one T; but the nearest he got was to buy the Corbet land at Ynysymaengwyn. His marriage to the vivacious Anna O'Meara, who was very popular in Tywyn, began to crumble.

Tywyn: beached dreams

He disliked her Catholic faith and declared that the father of her sixth child was a priest. As if in a Victorian Gothic novel, his lawyers drew up a banishment order, forbidding her to live within forty miles of his homes. Corbett cut her out of his will, too. After his death, Anna returned to Tywyn in 1906. It was like the home-coming of an exiled queen. She was welcomed by a brass band and rode in a procession led by a man on a white horse while the crowds cheered.

The heart of Tywyn is still St Cadfan's church, which has two wonders. The lesser one is the weeping knight, a stone effigy with an ever-glistening eye; and, if you like, you may imagine he is shedding tears over the incorrigible nature of mankind. The moisture of course, seeps out through capillary action in the stone.

The greater wonder is the Cadfan stone, thirteen centuries old, bearing the earliest words written in the Welsh language. It is a memorial to a much-loved wife. The inscription, 'Grief and Loss Remain', reaches out and touches us across the centuries.

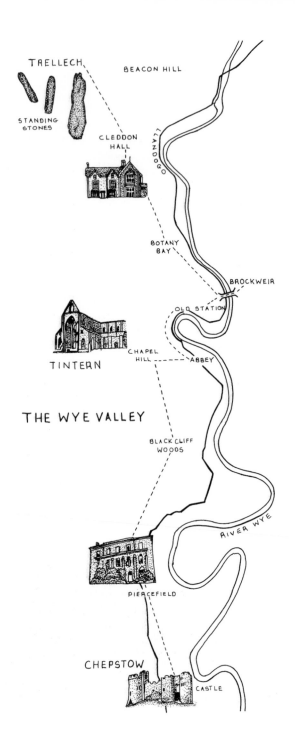

TRELLECH

BEACON HILL

STANDING STONES

CLEDDON HALL

BOTANY BAY

BROCKWEIR

OLD STATION

TINTERN

CHAPEL HILL

ABBEY

THE WYE VALLEY

BLACK CLIFF WOODS

RIVER WYE

PIERCEFIELD

CHEPSTOW

CASTLE

(LLANDOGO)

9. THE WYE VALLEY

In search of buried treasure

All of the Wye is lovely. I have tramped to its source, on the remote and windy slopes of Plynlimon, and I have explored long stretches of it in Wales and Herefordshire. For my *Wild Tracks* walk I chose the section of the mature river that winds in some grandeur from Llandogo to Chepstow by way of Tintern, a distance of about ten miles.

I admit I feel proprietorial, as well as lyrical, about the Wye. It is my native river. It flows close to the house where I was born and I feel I own a few gallons of it; though the river authority's lawyers might take a different view.

Actually I started above Llandogo, in the town of Trellech on the western side of the valley, enjoying the sweeping view of the landscape from the top of the mound, an old fortification. Trellech (there are several different spellings) was once one of the largest towns in Wales, but it never recovered its power after the battering it received in the Middle Ages. It was ravaged by the Black Death and heavily damaged in Owain Glyndwr's war of independence in the early years of the fifteenth century.

Trellech: stormy past

Sundial: information

The large church tells of the town's former significance. As I walked in I saw a sign on the door which indicated that the vicar was not only a gentleman, but a man with some experience of teetering godmothers. It read: 'Stiletto heels are very welcome, but beware of the grille in the centre aisle near the font. Bless you!'

Inside the church stands a seventeenth century stone sundial which does duty as an early tourist information service, showing the town's attractions. It has a rough carving of the mound, or motte, from which I had surveyed the countryside; and another carving of the trio of standing stones a short walk up the road. The nonsense tale about them says they possess enough occult energy to knock a man flat, but the truth is just as interesting: they were erected in the Bronze Age, about three thousand five hundred years ago, at a time when many standing stones and circles were raised in Britain.

Standing Stones: packing a punch?

The Virtuous Well: hope springs eternal

A third carving on the sundial directed me half a mile down the lane to the intriguing Virtuous Well which lies in a meadow within sight of the church, though it was here long before the church was built. It had its origins in pagan times and remains a place of pilgrimage. A belief in the healing properties of its water has endured. Wild flowers had been placed in the mossy alcove of the well and strips of cotton and silk had been tied to the twigs of the blackthorn and hazel trees beside the well. They fluttered in the breeze, like the prayer papers I have seen in Japanese temples, representing appeals for help, for a cure for sickness, speaking of the deep ache of hope.

On the way up the lane I saw two small children helping their grandfather to feed sheep in a meadow, such an idyllic scene that I hoped it would remain in their memories all their lives, a sunny day stored up to warm their old age. The path skirts Beacon Hill on the way to the river and took me through the woods and over a field, still wet with dew, in front of Cleddon Hall. This is where Bertrand Russell, Lord Russell the philosopher, was brought up in the 1870s. He was only two years old when his sister and then his mother died here of tuberculosis. His broken-hearted father died shortly afterwards. George Taylor, the owner of the hall, walked

Heartbreak: the tomb at Cleddon

me through a bluebell wood to show me the tomb in the grounds where Russell's mother and sister were laid to rest.

An old house like this does not seem inanimate. It is a store of memories, a witness of family fortunes. Cleddon Hall played a part in a shocking Victorian scandal. The Marquess of Blandford, Winston Churchill's uncle, arrived here with his mistress, Lady Aylesford. They were runaway lovers. The lady's husband was furious and so was the husband's friend, the Prince of Wales. Churchill's father, Lord Randolph Churchill, became involved in the dispute and was challenged to a duel by the Prince of Wales. Fortunately, tempers cooled, but Lord Randolph was cut out of high society for eight years.

I walked through Cleddon village, where Bertrand Russell's vivacious mother made such a stir with her progressive ideas on education, birth control, votes for women and equal pay. Welsh poppies were out on parade for me in vivid yellow clusters. This

Cleddon Hall: tales to tell

genuine native Welsh bloom really has a better claim to be the national flower than the upstart daffodil.

Through the trees, hundreds of feet above Llandogo, l glimpsed the Wye, coiled and shining in the valley. In the nineteenth century this tranquil and empty reach of river was crowded with sailing vessels and the busy port of Llandogo was full of water rats in human form. A nautical atmosphere still clings to the place and anchors are carved on some of the gravestones. The workhorses of the river were sailing sloops or barges known as trows (hence the pub called the Llandoger Trow on the stretch of waterfront known as the Welsh Back in Bristol). The bell of the last trow on the Wye is kept in the church here. Goods from Llandogo were traded as far as Italy.

I walked down the hill through the woodlands called Botany Bay – no one knows why – and took a detour, out of Wales and into England, across the ugly little bridge to Brockweir. It is a respectable little place now, but it had a misspent youth. Villager Barry Naylor told me that when it was a rough-and-ready trading and shipbuilding town it was full of cider houses. It was such a lawless place that the Moravian church was persuaded to build an outpost here in 1832 to save the village from its sins; and a combination of the church and the decline in the river trade has left

Moravian Church: sobering influence

Brockweir: horse haven

Brockweir a reformed character. One of its institutions now is the home for horses rescued from owners who have treated them cruelly. They are in the care of HAPPA, the Horses and Ponies Protection Association. Some are brought here having been neglected, half-starved or beaten. They stay for a few months until they are fit. It is sad to report that the flow of badly-treated horses is not decreasing.

I walked back across the bridge. Surely it was my imagination that the grass was just a shade greener? Along the riverbank I watched the railway signals changing, but there was no train. The old station at Tintern is a museum and children were having fun

Signals in the wood: Tintern

playing at signalman and stationmaster. The railway line here killed off the river barges and in its turn was axed in the Beeching reforms of the 1960s. The old posters at the station remind you of the adventures you could have by catching a train.

On the way to Tintern, I called at a vineyard and found the owner, Martin Rogers, ruefully examining his vines, damaged in the recent late frosts. But he was philosophical. His vineyard covers six acres and given a fair share of sunshine and an absence of frost produces a delicious white wine, ten thousand bottles in a good year.

I met Jim Simpson on the riverbank. He's something of a crusader, a man who loves the Wye and wants to make it easier for people to have access to it, as they did in the past. He does this by reclaiming the old boat slipways which lie buried under the river-bank. Old photographs and maps provide plenty of evidence that the slipways existed and Jim employs mechanical diggers to uncover them. He told me he believes strongly in our right to mess about in boats and was popular with some people for his direct action ... but not with everybody.

Slipway to the Wye

In the grand opera of this stretch of the Wye the chief performer is the Cistercian abbey at Tintern, a ruin made for our eternal entertainment and contemplation. It certainly plays a star-ring role in the cult of the picturesque. During the eighteenth century, when tourism was in its infancy, a debate began on how landscapes should be properly appreciated. It was not enough simply to look at a natural scene: it had to be viewed as a framed picture, as an artistic creation.

Tintern Abbey: pleasures of melancholy

The Reverend William Gilpin, a vicar from the New Forest, wrote a book in 1770 called *Observations on the River Wye*. It became a tourist bible, advocating that the countryside should be examined 'by the rules of picturesque beauty'. Ruins were considered enhancers of landscape; and those at Tintern were especially valued as aids to the spectator's enjoyment, setting off the limestone cliffs and curves of the river. Actually, Gilpin was a little disappointed with Tintern. Looking around, he suggested that the ruin would be more picturesque if parts of it were knocked down with a mallet, if it were ruined a little more. Some visitors thought the ruins were not gloomy enough to inspire the proper feeling of melancholy. Others found, to their distaste, that the ruins were peopled by ghastly crones and poor folk; and many of these ragged bundles sprang to life and offered themselves as guides.

An eighteenth-century visitor, more after my own heart, said the best way to enjoy Tintern was to take a picnic of wine and cold meat, and hire a harpist from Chepstow.

Across the road from the abbey, on Chapel Hill, I explored another ruin, the old parish church. The whole area was a glorious wildflower show, a mass of buttercup and speedwell, greater

Chapel Hill, Tintern: men of iron

stitchwort and forget-me-not, tufted vetch and herb robert, bistort, red campion and, the favourite of the bees, yellow archangel. A number of tombs are those of Victorian men of substance, reminders of industry and wealth. Some are monuments to the owners of ironworks and the nearby wire works that produced the first transatlantic telegraph cable.

The last stretch of the journey lay over a meadow and onto the track through Blackcliff Woods. It was heavenly with the scent of wild garlic, really quite pungent. I was soon back again in the world of the picturesque, walking a path fashioned two hundred years ago by the imaginative Valentine Morris on his Piercefield estate. He designed this magical tour to lead his guests to cunningly-sited vantage points for picturesque scenes; and at one place he would fire a cannon to delight them with the echo. There was a grandstand view from the Eagle's Nest. (Today the first Severn Bridge lies in the distance.) Below me lay the ground on which, in the Middle Ages, stood a leper colony. Good-hearted monks used to row down with the tide to deliver food.

I walked down the 365 steps built by the Duke of Beaufort and restored by the Wye Valley Preservation Society. It is an

'Steep woods and lofty cliffs' – Wordsworth on the Wye

adventurous trip through trees which looked like pantomime scenery, all gnarled and snaking roots, and across little bridges set among the crags. Better down than up.

Across the river was the cliff known as Wintour's Leap. The story behind it is a pretty tall tale. Sir John Wintour, who fought on the Cavaliers' side in the Civil War, was said to have jumped his horse from the cliff and into the river to escape his pursuers. Since it is a drop of more than two hundred feet it is more likely that Sir John found a path and scrambled down.

Piercefield was Valentine Morris's pleasure ground. But things went wrong for him. He became involved in politics and gambling – hard to know which was worse – and lost his money, eventually fleeing to the West Indies, where he died in poverty. In the end the house began to crumble and then suffered a terminal indignity of being used as a wartime bombing target. Though battered, part of it still stands. The parkland became Chepstow racecourse in 1921. The great Gordon Richards loved the place: he once rode eleven consecutive winners here.

Deep in the woods I came to a large hole which, at first, I thought might be a bomb crater. In fact it was one of a number of

Piercefield House: survivor

holes which remain as a memorial to the strange quest of Dr Orville Ward Owen, a physician from Detroit.

He believed passionately that Shakespeare's plays were the work of Francis Bacon. To help him prove his theories he built a contraption of spools with a canvas belt a thousand feet long. To this he stuck Elizabethan texts in an attempt to unravel a code he believed they contained. He declared that Bacon's manuscripts were stored in sixty-six iron boxes, one of which contained Shakespeare's head, in a cave somewhere near Chepstow.

He was so convincing that he persuaded several people to finance his search and in 1909 dug for months in the cliff caves near Chepstow Castle. Finding nothing, he then announced that the boxes lay in the bed of the Wye and persuaded another backer to finance an expedition in 1911 in which a dam was built and engineers struggled for months against floods. The doctor gave up and went home to America, but throughout the 1920s his American disciples excavated around the castle. They also dug in the woods, flying the Stars and Stripes over their excavations, in their long and hopeless search for the sixty-six iron chests.

I climbed down a fallen tree to the bottom of one of these holes and, pondering the obsession of Dr Ward Owen, gave the leafy earth a couple of stabs with my walking stick, half-hoping, I suppose, that I would hit a rusty box.

Chepstow Castle: my finishing post

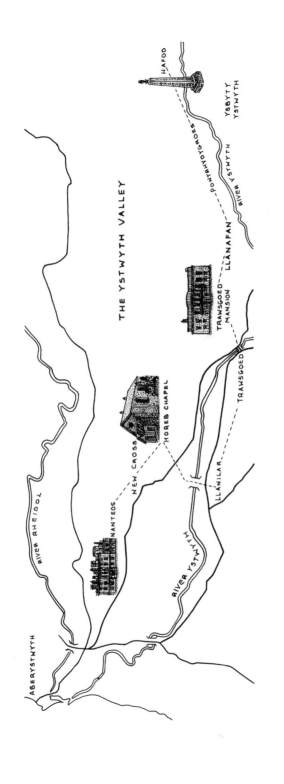

THE YSTWYTH VALLEY

ABERYSTWYTH

RIVER RHEIDOL

RIVER YSTWYTH

NANTEOS

NEW CROSS

HOREB CHAPEL

LLANILAR

TRAWSGOED

TRAWSGOED
MANSION

LLANAFAN

PONTRHYDYGROES

RIVER YSTWYTH

YSBYTY
YSTWYTH

HAFOD

10. THE YSTWYTH VALLEY

The silvery way

Ahead of me, as I set out to walk the fourteen miles from Nanteos to Hafod, lay the valley of the Ystwyth, its forests and spectacular narrow gorges.

This is a district of Cardiganshire where men built grand houses and ruled their estates as if they were private kingdoms. My starting place, the Palladian mansion of Nanteos, lies at the end of a lovely tree-lined avenue two miles east of Aberystwyth. It was built in 1739 by Thomas Powell, who, like others, made his fortune from lead mining and property. In its heyday his estate encompassed 186 farms.

Mansions like Nanteos added much grace to the Welsh landscape. The squires who built them were rarely outsiders. They usually had Welsh ancestry, many were Welsh-speaking and most fitted easily into their locality. A good number had interests beyond hunting, banqueting and claret, paid their respects to Welsh culture and were enthusiastic about architecture, furniture and painting.

Nanteos: idylls and storms

122

The passion that some of them had for gardening, tree planting and the design of parks led to an enhancement of the countryside which we enjoy today. Nanteos is especially handsome, its elegant facade set against a backdrop of trees in the sublime landscape between the rivers Rheidol and Ystwyth.

I met Janet Joel in the front hall. She visits Nanteos as often as she can because she is simply in love with it. When she was a child her aunt owned the house and Janet spent idyllic days playing in the grounds and the numerous rooms, the Macaw Room, Damask Room, Japanese Room, the Christmas Room and so on. It became her magic house and she is the happy prisoner of its spell. Indeed, she has given the name of Nanteos to her own home thirty miles away.

'I have so many lovely memories I can't keep away,' she said, looking dreamily around her. 'As soon as I arrive all my cares just disappear.'

In the 1860s the squire was William Powell, a former Tory MP, very proud of his prize cattle. His heir, George, was rather a disappointment to him: he was a poet, an admirer of the Marquis de Sade and a hater of hunting, shooting and fishing. When George invited his friend, the poet Algernon Swinburne, to stay, the old squire would not have the man in the house. It didn't help that the outrageous Swinburne brought with him his mistress, a five times married circus rider. George and Swinburne went out drinking and released the squire's prize bull. The story goes that the furious father thrust a gun into his son's hand and ordered him to prove himself a man – to go out and shoot something. So George went out. He found the prize bull and shot it dead.

George inherited the estate in 1878 and with it the Nanteos Cup, a wooden bowl reputed to be the Holy Grail, the goblet used at the Last Supper. As such it was credited with being the instrument of miraculous cures. Pilgrims flocked to Nanteos to see it and the sick gnawed pieces from it, like beavers. In fact, it was a commonplace medieval cup and there is no mention of it before 1857.

In November 1918 people gathered at Nanteos to celebrate the end of the First World War when news arrived of the death of the heir to the estate. Lieutenant William Powell, Welsh Guards, had been killed in France on November 6, the last week of the fighting. It was the end of the dynasty.

The hunting hounds of Nanteos were kept in kennels some

Woodman spares that tree

distance from the house and the buildings have been converted into a lovely cottage. This is the home of Bob Shaw, an amiable bushy-bearded craftsman, lover of woodlands and teacher of woodland management. He showed me around the stretch of trees he owns and the workshop where he makes furniture, gates and fences. I enjoyed watching him at work in a glade. No zizz of power tools disturbs the birdsong because Bob doesn't use them. He works only with traditional implements and gently-whirring foot-powered lathes. 'I'm so lucky to be able to do this for a living,' he said.

Along the road in New Cross, in Horeb chapel, I visited the grave of that remarkable writer Caradoc Evans. He died aged sixty-seven in 1940, having revelled in his reputation as 'the best hated man in Wales'. He was a bitter fellow and the chief object of his scorn – expressed in notorious books like *My People* and *My Neighbours* – was Nonconformity.

To his mind the chapels reeked of hypocrisy. John Ceredig Davies was a boy when Caradoc stalked the village and remembered that people were afraid to speak to him, fearing they would be ridiculed in his writing. He told me that Caradoc used to listen to the sermons in the chapel, making comments while nonchalantly and scandalously sitting with his feet up on the pew in front. One Sunday the preacher called him 'a stink on the map of humanity'

Horeb: grave of the scourge

and Caradoc, who liked to dish out abuse but could not always take it, walked out.

'Bury me lightly,' reads the inscription on his gravestone on the hillside, 'so that the small rain may reach my face and the fluttering of the butterfly shall not escape my ear.'

It's as if he's still listening, still ready to dip his pen in bile.

The path to Llanilar affords exhilarating views, but in one part the landscape was spoiled for me by the wind turbines in the distance. What irritating, absurd and ugly things they are.

I crossed the springy toy suspension bridge over the sparkling Ystwyth and walked to Llanilar along the broad path on which the railway used to run. It was closed in the 1970s, but a four-mile stretch of it is being rebuilt by steam enthusiasts: yet another of the revived little railways of Wales that do so well. Old railways never die. They become train sets for grown ups, for Members of The Honourable Brotherhood of the Oily Rag. In a farmyard not far away I found engines of a different kind, agricultural machines used for threshing in the early years of the century, and lovingly restored by Glyn James and his son, Wyre.

Gleaming antique

I slowed my pace to a stroll as I passed through the woods on the south side of the river. One of the glades had won a gold award in the Royal Welsh Show. The Forestry Commission has planted it with North American red oak, Japanese red cedar, Japanese larch, Norway maple and Corsican pine both to improve the range of trees and to see how new varieties fare in the market.

It was encouraging to see some young and vigorous elms, particularly as Dutch elm disease has wiped out every mature elm in the county. Richard Thompson, a forester, said that the disease is not necessarily a complete catastrophe. 'Before they reach fifteen feet these elms produce fertile seed. The outlook is fairly favourable. Disease hit the elms hard in Roman times, but they came back in good numbers.' Foresters have to take the long view. For a while we watched blue tits and pied flycatchers flitting busily in and out of nesting boxes. Richard told me that the finicky blue tits like boxes with 28mm holes while the flycatchers much prefer openings of 32mm.

Reaching the bottom of the valley, I crossed the Ystwyth again and entered the Trawsgoed estate which was owned for more than four hundred years by the Vaughan family and grew to forty thousand acres in the nineteenth century. During the Second World War the National Gallery sent seventy paintings here to keep them safe from bombs. The old central heating system made the air in the house too dry and blankets were hung up everywhere and sprayed with water to achieve the right level of humidity.

The historian Gerald Morgan, who has written a book about the Vaughans, regaled me with stories of this remarkable family, some of whom were solid stanchions of society, while others were ruined by 'slow horses and fast women.'

A gravestone half-concealed in the long grass of Llanafan

Trawsgoed: family seat

Gardener's art: Trawsgoed

churchyard records that Joseph Butler, a gamekeeper, was shot by
a poacher in 1868. The background of this murder, which started
a great manhunt, was the election of November of that year.

Feelings ran high between the Tories and Liberals as the
Liberals made their first important breakthrough. The Tory land-
lord, Lord Lisburne – Edward Vaughan of Trawsgoed – lost his
seat. That night the unfortunate gamekeeper was shot in Dolfor
Woods by William Richards. In spite of a large reward, the local
people closed ranks around him: in their eyes he was a hero in the
struggle between the gentry and the poor. After months on the run,
hiding and never betrayed, he fled to Liverpool disguised as a
woman and took ship for New York. There he was given sanctuary by two Cardiganshire men and settled near Jackson, Ohio. His
sweetheart, Bet Morgan, was smuggled out to him and they lived
the rest of their lives in Ohio. William Richards died in 1921, aged
eighty, far from the seething emotions of the Welsh countryside of
1868. Those people in Cardiganshire, who knew he was in
America, kept the secret for more than fifty years.

The valley grew narrower now. Along this stretch lie the shafts
and spoil heaps of numerous mines. Lead and silver were mined
here for centuries. The Grogwynion mine, high up to my left, was

Spent riches: old mines at Grogwynion

worked by British slaves in Roman times. Some of the mines were hugely profitable and in 1624 one of them sent 3,000 ounces of silver to the Royal Mint. In the 1860s Wales produced nearly 28,000 tons of lead ore and several thousand people worked in mines around Plynlimon.

In the seventeenth and eighteenth centuries this was wild and lawless country. Twenty-seven condemned criminals were offered a pardon if they worked seven years in the mines. After the first day's gruelling work one of them said he would rather have been hanged. On more than one occasion dragoons and fusiliers were called in to scatter rioting mobs of miners armed with scythes and pitchforks. Scheming owners sometimes incited mobs to attack their rivals. A cleric complained that so many people were either bandits or debauched that it was dangerous for any minister to attempt to hold a service. And it was noted that in one chapel the pews were cleared out and men engaged in wrestling bouts, egged on by cheering women.

But gradually respect for law and education prevailed. Drunkenness and rioting faded away. In Pontrhydygroes, the capital of the Cardiganshire Klondike, chapels exerted a strong influence and mining communities made a determined effort to

Ystwyth Gorge: reward for the intrepid

educate themselves. Books gained ground over beer. In the 1860s petitions from miners opposed the opening of more ale houses.

But before reaching Pontrhydygroes I tackled an exciting and rugged stage of my journey, a scramble through the woods and along some precipice paths. I had a guide, Richard Wilson, who runs walking tours in these parts. He took me through the forest and out onto a high rock with a wonderful view of the Ystwyth gorge and waterfalls. 'It's not often seen by walkers,' Richard said. 'This viewpoint is hard to reach unless you have special knowledge. And you also need an intrepid spirit.'

I entered the third great estate of my walk, Hafod, the creation of Thomas Johnes. It is the setting of an astonishing and tragic story. Johnes arrived in 1783 with his wife and daughter, dreaming of building a garden of Eden in this forbidding upland wilderness. He spent his fortune creating a paradise beside the wild river, laid out a lovely park and planted several million trees, largely oak and larch. His mansion, designed partly by Nash, was a temple of culture, a storehouse of great paintings. His library was a collection of treasures. His printing press was famous for its fine work. Writers and artists streamed in to gaze at this wonder of the picturesque. As a farmer, Johnes tried new crops and breeds, not

Hafod: vanished glory

always with success, and made great efforts to see that his tenants were contented.

'It was his Xanadu,' said Jennie Macve, who showed me one of his scenic walks.

Yet it seemed that malevolent fates conspired against Thomas Johnes, as if envious of the beauty he had created. In 1807 his house of treasures was burnt down. He rebuilt it, but the old magic had gone, so much had been lost.

Four years later, his gifted daughter, Mariamne, as lovely as her name, died aged twenty-six. Her heartbroken father commissioned Sir Francis Chantrey to make a poignant marble monument, a depiction of the family together for the last time. The sculpture showed Mariamne's palette and brushes, a lyre and the music of Handel she loved best. But her father had spent all of his money on his estate and could not afford to pay for the memorial; so his friends did.

It was brought to the church at Hafod. Touching and beautiful, it attracted many visitors over the years. But the fates hadn't finished with Thomas Johnes.

In 1932 the church caught fire and blazing roof timbers fell on the statue of Mariamne. The heat and the water of the firemen's

The last bitter blow

hoses shattered the marble almost beyond recognition.

The once-beautiful sculpture, reduced to rubble, is still there. In it lies the face of Thomas Johnes. The expression is of pain and suffering. It is unforgettably haunting.

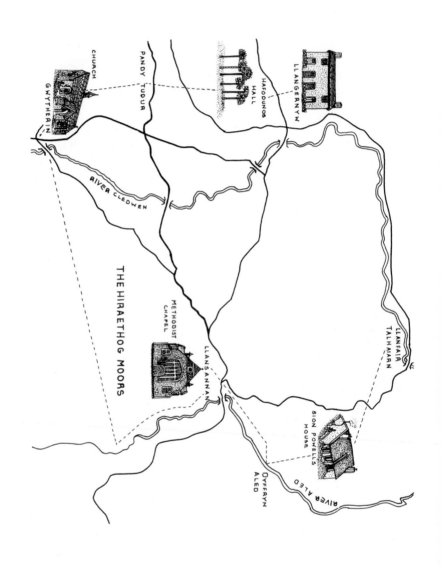

CHUACH

GWYTHERIN

PANDY TUDUR

HAFODUNOS

HALL

LLANGERNYW

RIVER CLEDWEN

THE HIRAETHOG MOORS

METHODIST
CHAPEL

LLANSANNAN

LLANFAIR
TALHAIARN

SION POWELL'S
HOUSE

DYFFRYN
ALED

RIVER ALED

11. THE HIRAETHOG MOORS

Poets, quarrels, sheep and the Kaiser's men

Between the Conwy Valley and the Vale of Clwyd in north east Wales lies a quiet district of villages and moors, off the beaten path, not well known and full of charming and secluded places: another of those parts of Wales that invites you to believe you are an explorer.

I started off in pretty Llangernyw, in the Gallen valley, and my first call was at the boyhood home of the local hero, Sir Henry Jones. His story reads like one of those improving Victorian tales of steadfastness, a determined struggle to rise from humble beginnings. He was born in Llangernyw in 1852, was apprenticed at twelve to his shoemaker father and, self-taught at first, went on to scale the academic heights. He became an outstanding teacher, education reformer and philosopher. After the founding of the University of Wales he organised the financing of higher education through a penny tax on ratepayers. Later he made a career as an educator and author in Scotland.

'Wake up, Henry': cobbler's cottage, Llangernyw

The tiny cobbler's cottage in Llangernyw is maintained as a museum and contains young Henry's shoemaking tools and iron bedstead. In a side wall is the small window on which the village policeman tapped at one o'clock in the morning, the signal for Henry to rise, light his candle and immerse himself in his books.

The people are still proud of their golden boy and a few years ago wrote and staged a musical of his life, a sort of 'Henry Jones – Superstar.' Indeed, the village is proud of all its scholars and poets, men who laboured hard for their learning, like J.T. Jones, a workman's son who translated *Hamlet* into Welsh.

Henry Jones's cousin, Robert Roberts, who is buried in Llangernyw churchyard, was another remarkable character, known in Wales as 'the Great Scholar'. He trained as an Anglican priest but in 1861 was sacked for preaching while drunk at Corwen. He went to Australia to dig for gold and began to compile a great dictionary. It was never published. He returned to Wales in 1875, worked as a teacher and died in 1885 of an overdose of laudanum. His autobiography, a well-drawn portrait of life in Victorian Wales, was published in 1923, a long time after his death, and it was this that brought his name to a wide public.

The churchyard at Llangernyw is the scene of the downfall of the irrepressible Harri William, a schoolmaster, ventriloquist and prankster. He once stopped some farmhands leading a horse-drawn cart loaded with hay and made it appear that a child was crying in the middle of the load. They searched frantically while Harri laughed. But he went too far when a coffin was being lowered into a grave here, making it appear that the deceased was speaking. There was consternation, Harri was found out – and sacked from his teaching job.

The yew tree in the churchyard, incidentally, is a true patriarch, the oldest tree in Wales, more than four thousand years old. You work out its age by measuring its circumference. The church used to hide its central heating oil tank in its trunk, but moved it elsewhere when it was found that the tree was so old and majestic.

Half a mile or so out of Llangernyw I came to Hafodunos Hall. It belongs to another age, a magnificent Gothic country house of stone and red brick designed by Sir Gilbert Scott and built in the 1860s for a Liverpool merchant. Above it rises a handsome clock tower and there is a grand conservatory and an octagonal billiard room. I could imagine the army of servants needed to run it. In its time it has been a squire's house, a girls' school, a college and a

Grand old man: Llangernyw

Hafodunos Hall: rich man's castle

Lost!

retirement home. It seemed to me, as I passed by, like an old and eccentric recluse, stranded by time.

The first Hafodunos house on this site was owned by John Lloyd who, in 1774, was present at the opening of the tomb of Edward I in Westminster Abbey. When he saw the King's face he spat upon it. Why? Because he believed the untrue story that Edward had ordered the slaughter of Welsh bards in the thirteenth century.

The footpath wound through the grounds below the house. In the golden days of these gardens exotic plants grew in profusion; but without the attention of platoons of gardeners nature has reasserted itself and the place has become an overgrown tangle. It reminded me of a tropical forest, the sun finding its way through the thick tree cover. I half-expected to see monkeys swinging through the trees and crocodiles basking beside the tumbling river. The path disappeared in the thick undergrowth and I had to admit I was lost in this Welsh jungle.

Scrambling out at last, I was relieved to see the sky and open countryside again. As a distant navigation mark there stood a distinctive avenue of monkey puzzle trees, one of the glories of the old Hafodunos estate, like a row of bottle brushes against the sky. Over a hillslope I came to the second village on my walk. Its old name was Pandy Budur, which means the dirty mill, but the people changed it to Pandy Tudur, which looked much better on their headed notepaper. In common with other upland villages it has the problems of too many holiday homes and too few young people. But it still has energy and the chapel is the heart of community life. When the bakery closed, the villagers converted it into three business units, a house and a flat, an investment in the future.

The pleasant footpath out of Pandy Tudur took me through a rockery and a garden and soon I was on high ground, walking beside rolling green pastures; and I imagined the thoughtful sheep counting me as I went by.

High above the valley, the farmland gave way to brown moorland, to reeds, marshy patches and rough pasture, and long, lonely paths, whipped by the wind. A litter of rusting, abandoned farm machinery and a deserted farm building contributed to the sense of desolation. I had the moors to myself. The top of the hill, as always, offered its rewarding view and the inviting sanctuary of the valley below.

Hafodunos: monkey puzzle landmark

Gwytherin: spirit of renewal

I walked down to the isolated village of Gwytherin. Its church honours the memory of the remarkable St Winifred, whose head, legend says, was lopped off by a frustrated seducer and was stuck on again by her uncle, St Beuno. Her venerated bones attracted many pilgrims who, of course, brought money. They were coveted by the monks of Shrewsbury who took them away and installed them in their abbey where they immediately became a source of considerable profit.

Twenty years ago Gwytherin was almost lifeless. Everything had closed: pub, post office, shop, school and church. But the local people decided to put their community back on its feet. The church has been reconsecrated and the pub is back in business: two vital sources of community life restored. The village feels like a village again. It has won the best-kept village prize twice. The telephone box is a centre of civic pride, regularly cleaned and furnished with flowers, an ashtray and a litter bin; and the public ty bach looks like a flower stall. In the heart of the village a stone marks the rebirth and the new spirit of the community.

As I was talking to some of the local people, a flock of sheep came down from the hills, at high speed and full of complaints, and looked as if they would bowl me over if I didn't step aside.

Sheep jam

Sheep were the centre of attention in Gwytherin that day. The court of estrays was meeting to sort out and adjudicate on the stray sheep in the district. It is a ritual that dates from medieval times. The judges, experienced farmers, were sworn in, taking the oath in a ceremony conducted in ornate Welsh, sealing the oath by kissing the bible. Strays, brought down from the moors, are all earmarked, but they may have changed hands a few times and the judges' task was to examine the earmarks and decide who owns them. Any unclaimed sheep are auctioned and the money pays for a shepherds' dinner; pie, perhaps. The court is a serious business but there is a genial social side to it, a chance to meet for a drink and a gossip.

I climbed out of Gwytherin and up to the broad back of the Hiraethog moors. It was not too difficult to imagine how hostile this moorland could be in winter. I had a good view of a striking landmark, a shooting lodge known as 'the wooden palace'. It was built in Norway, dismantled, shipped and reassembled in 1913 on the bleak hill. Now the wind tears at it, gradually shaking it to pieces.

I followed the path to the upper reaches of the River Aled and looked down into the gorge at spectacular waterfalls. An extraordinary number of gifted men were born in this district, part of

The Aled Valley: spectacular

Llansannan parish, and grew up to be giants of the written word. A house nearby was the home of Henry Rees, the great nineteenth-century religious leader, and his brother William, known as Gwilym Hiraethog, the radical writer and editor who had a strong influence on journalism in Wales. We shall hear more of them a little later.

Nearby is the birthplace of the Elizabethan scholar William Midleton, a poet who was the first to publish a collection of Welsh verse. He was also an adventurer and privateer, scourge of the Spaniards; and also the first man to smoke that new-found weed tobacco at the court of Queen Elizabeth. Not far away is the house where William Salesbury translated the New Testament into Welsh in 1567; and in the neighbourhood, too, is the birthplace of Tudur Aled, a giant among bards, who lived from 1465-1525 and who lies buried in Carmarthen, not beneath some noble shady oak but under the Tesco supermarket.

A narrow, rather secret lane brought me to a cottage in a peaceful corner, the home of Nora Kirienko. She served tea in the garden and told me her remarkable tale.

Her husband, Vasili, was caught up in the whirlwinds of Russia and Europe at war. He fled first from the Ukraine when Russia was engulfed in revolution in 1917 and made his way to Poland. He fled to Britain as the Nazis tightened their grip and met and married Nora, an Englishwoman. His only possession when he arrived was a silver teaspoon, given to him by a Jewish family who had befriended him and who later died in a Nazi extermination camp. After the war he took Nora to Czechoslovakia. But they had to flee the Communists and at last made their way to this remote part of Wales where they settled. Vasili became a builder and constructed several houses in the neighbourhood. Nora, now a widow, still lives in the house that was their happy sanctuary; and uses the silver teaspoon every day.

In Llansannan I visited the two chapels that stand as monuments to a bitter religious quarrel. The Methodist chapel honours Henry Rees. The Independent chapel remembers his brother Gwilym Hiraethog. They quarrelled over a Methodist farmer who, on business in Chester, was told that his wife had been taken ill and set off for home in Llansannan. He arrived on Sunday morning and for this crime, travelling on the Sabbath, was sternly expelled from the Methodist congregation.

Gwilym Hiraethog and others were appalled at such inhumanity and left with him. Later the Methodists built a chapel in Henry's memory, and the Independents a chapel in honour of Gwilym. Only people in cities think that country life is sleepy. Passions have always run deep in villages.

Llansannan is proud of its literary connections and has erected a white stone monument, a statue of a little girl with perfect hands by Sir William Goscombe John. It commemorates its five local heroes: Henry Rees, Gwilym Hiraethog, Tudur Aled, William Salesbury and Iorwerth Glanaled.

The war memorial in Llansannan lists not only the men of the village who were

Llansannan: writers' block

A WASANAETHODD

BRYN GOLEU

PTE A. ROBERTS   MOSTYN UCHA
  H. ROBERTS   TRYFAN ISA
  J. ROBERTS   SARACENS HEAD
  J. ROBERTS   PANT GLAS
  T. ROBERTS
  J. ROBERTS   TOP LLAN
  R. ROBERTS
  P. ROBERTS   CHWIBREN UCHA
  R. ROBERTS   BONT CARREG FAWR
CAPT. C.D. SMART M.C.   COVERPOINT
PTE J. SYMMONDS   ALED TERRACE
  J.B. THOMAS   BRYN'R ORSEDD
  T. THOMAS

Heroes and cricket

killed in the First World War but also those who went to fight and came back – heaven knows they suffered, too. And there is affection in the description of them as the 'boys' of Llansannan. Their addresses are given, too, and show that some of the village houses were built by a man who adored cricket. Captain Smart lived at Coverpoint and Private Brassington at Square Leg. Amid the horrors of war how they must have dreamed of cricket and Llansannan.

I walked through the woods of the Aled valley and, watching a buzzard at work, made my way up the slope to Dyffryn Aled, a modern home built on the site of a mansion which graced this attractive valley.

The owner, Howard Bibby, a retired naval officer, told me the tale of the attempted escape by German prisoners of war confined here in 1915. The men kept at Dyffryn Aled were naval officers, captured in 1914, and some of them, because of their experience and knowledge, were of great importance. They hatched a daring plan to escape from the mansion and make their way to the Great Orme at Llandudno where they would be picked up by a submarine. They gave the details of the plan to an interned German civilian who was repatriated in 1914; and confirmation of the rendezvous was sent to them in code in relatives' letters.

Three officers broke out of the camp in August 1915 and walked through the night to reach Llandudno twenty miles away. They ate a full Welsh breakfast in a cafe and, that night, went to keep their appointment on the headland. The submarine was there but the nature of the rocks meant that the escapers and the submarine crew were hidden from each other. As arranged, the prisoners and the submarine tried again during the next two nights. They were tantalizingly close but they failed to make contact. Dejected, they were soon spotted by sharp-eyed residents in Llandudno and arrested.

On the home run now, I passed the house where Sion Powell lived. He was a minor poet more famous for his curious laundry

Llanfair Talhaiarn: poet's corner

habits than his verse. Not liking to change his shirt, he kept it on and every now and then simply lay in a stream for a few minutes.

Over the hill – and there lay Llanfair Talhaiarn. It was once the home of John Jones, a nineteenth-century lyric poet, wit and architect who helped to build the Crystal Palace in London. He was not chapel and not especially sober and found his enjoyment in the company of drinking men.

'What do you Welsh use your language for?' a foreign visitor once asked him.

'To praise ourselves and attack each other,' he replied.

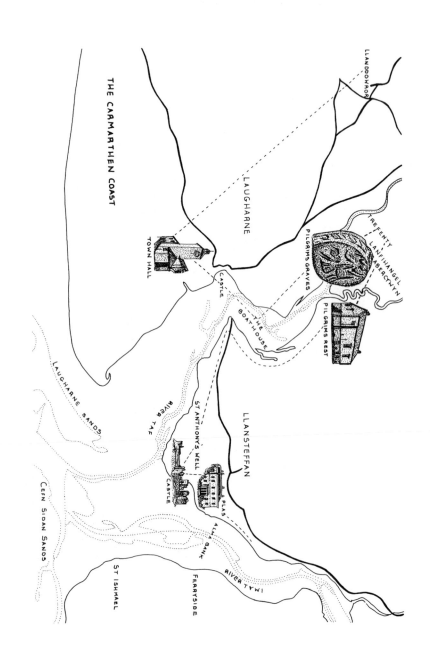

THE CARMARTHEN COAST

LLANDDOWROR

LAUGHARNE

TREFENTY
LANFIHANGEL
ABERCWYN

PILGRIMS GRAVES

TOWN HALL

CASTLE
THE BOATHOUSE

PILGRIMS REST

LAUGHARNE SANDS

RIVER TAF

ST ANTHONY'S WELL

LLANSTEFFAN

CEFN SIDAN SANDS

CASTLE

PLAS

ALMA BANK

ST ISHMAEL

FERRYSIDE

RIVER TYWI

12. THE CARMARTHEN COAST

Walking on the water

In most parts of Wales people enjoy the amiable conceit that their village, their valley, their bro, is singular and special, charmingly different from any other; and also something of a secret divulged to a fortunate few.

They are all, of course, perfectly right. Wales is a wonderfully tessellated land and, for all the explorations of it down the centuries, it remains a place of piquant discoveries. Any walk is an enjoyable peeling of the onion and I have to agree with the people of Llansteffan and Laugharne, and those who inhabit the neighbouring countryside, that theirs is a delightful and different district. I like its whimsical air.

This is an area where rivers mingle with the sea – the salty sniff of estuaries combines with the rich smell of woodland and hay. I set off in the bright slanting light of morning, aiming to walk from one lovely estuary to another.

I headed south along the western foreshore of the Tywi river. The tide was out and sailing craft rested on their bilge keels on shining hillslopes of mud. In the misty distance, noble on its crag, loomed the profile of Llansteffan Castle. I soon skirted around a

Landmark: Llansteffan Castle

145

Pilglas: 'Off to Philadelphia in the morning'

curly worm of a creek and would have thought little of it had not Terry James told me of its history. Pilglas, the creek is called, and although to my eye there was barely room in it to swing a coracle around, it was for some years an embarkation point for intrepid and fearful Welsh people sailing to a new life in North America.

The fifty or so who set off in the 113-ton Carmarthen-built brig *Priscilla* in 1820 had a terrible time of it in the north Atlantic. The ship was not in good condition, not unusual in those days, and was dismasted in a storm. It struggled gamely back to Swansea under jury rig after an abortive voyage of fifty-eight days, its wretched passengers only half alive. It sank shortly after it reached safety.

Sailing vessels used to thread their way into Pilglas to discharge their cargoes of limestone at the kiln whose ruins still stand. Small ships also came with Gwendraeth Valley coal which was unloaded onto carts waiting on the road above the creek. The last collier, the *Primrose*, traded into the 1940s and her bones lie in the mud of Pilglas like a memorial.

Terry James also told me about the 'battle of Alma Bank' in 1864, a bitter clash between the seine netters and the coracle men who fished the Tywi. The Alma sand bank, which lies between Ferryside and Llansteffan, was the chosen battleground as the angry men, some supported by their wives, waded into each other. Yells and curses, bloody noses, broken bones: the battle was an ugly spectacle. A Ferryside woman was wounded by gunfire. It was said in the yarning later that one of the coracle men did not stop running until he reached America.

The cottages of Llansteffan looked lovely in the sunshine, as if wearing fresh bright shirts to have their pictures taken. The village is a place for holidays of the quiet, slightly old-fashioned kind, for walks, pottering on the beach, sailing, shrimping, sandcastling, reading in the sun, visiting the pubs and thinking about lunch.

It had its heyday as a resort in the first half of this century. Miners and their families came in force, particularly from the Rhondda and from the Sirhowy valley of Gwent. It was popular with Swindon railwaymen, too. Many arrived by train at Ferryside and a dozen boats ferried them across the estuary. There were frequent arguments between the parish council and the ferry owners, the council demanding at one stage that the ferrymen should remain sober.

Before the First World War almost every house in the village took in visitors and you could get a room for ten shillings a week. Bedrooms were subdivided by blankets hung from the ceiling. It was common for holidaymakers to bring their own food, for economy's sake, and the landladies prepared and cooked it. Old photographs show the streets crowded with trippers, many of the women carrying parasols, anxious to avoid an unfashionable tan.

The whole month of August was a festival in this jolly Welsh costa, a glorious escape for hard-working people, for men who laboured underground. The place rang with laughter. The pubs were always busy and, after hours, people would carry on drinking at their lodgings – rum with milk was a favourite tipple. Always ready for an impromptu noson lawen, they sang and recited into the small hours. And some of the pubs would be open at six o'clock in the morning!

Part of Llansteffan's fun was, and is, the election for the mock-mayor, a festival of serious nonsense. People still talk of the uproarious election in the 1930s when one of the leading contenders promised in his manifesto a daily weather forecast for shoemakers and his opponent pledged to stock the bay with mermaids to bring bachelors into the town.

I had a chat with Des Cridland, a Carmarthen cattle drover, who had been mayor ten years running. The proud wearer of the mayoral hat and scarlet robes, he was being driven around the town in an open car. Things have been arranged so that, in the hilarious climax to the election, Mr Cridland scrapes ahead of his rival thanks to the vote from Patagonia, telephoned through at the last minute.

'You have to have a character for this job,' he said, modestly, 'and maybe I am the last of the characters.'

The artist Ozi Osmond, who does duty as the mayor's chauffeur, is a contented resident of Llansteffan. 'Rivers and the sea,' he mused, summing up its attractions, 'the rhythm of the tides, the light over the water ... a magical place that exercises a strong hold over people.'

Plas Llansteffan: bookman's rest

Not far from my path stood Plas Llansteffan, retirement home of the great Welsh doctor Sir John Williams. Born in Carmarthenshire in 1840, brought up by his determined widowed mother, he rose from humble beginnings to become Queen Victoria's gynaecologist. It was the continuing of a Welsh connection, for the Queen's own birth had been supervised by David Daniel Davis, of Carmarthenshire.

Devoted to Welsh culture and the idea of Wales, Sir John dreamed of seeing the founding of the National Library of Wales. To this end, he acquired the magnificent collection of books and manuscripts that became the very heart of the library which was chartered in 1907 and opened on its present site in Aberystwyth in 1916.

Llansteffan Castle: grandstand view

Llansteffan castle is handsome enough in appearance, but, militarily, was never a difficult nut to crack: it seems that every siege of it was successful. From the ramparts stretches a splendid view of Carmarthen Bay and the sweep of the notorious Cefn Sidan sands, where hundreds of sailing ships were wrecked. One of the last was the four-masted *Paul*, of Hamburg, in 1925. On the other side of the estuary the village of St Ishmael was overwhelmed by a storm early in the seventeenth century.

I had a long and splashy walk over the estuary sands to see Bill Hill at work. A giant figure, in shorts and waders, he was picking out the fish trapped in his stake nets set out on the water's edge. Bill, who holds the only netting licence this side of the Tywi, runs a restaurant in Llansteffan and his freshly-caught fish is popular with his customers. As he said: 'Fishing isn't so bad on a warm day like today, but it's a job and not a hobby, and it is not so much fun having to get up at three in the morning, when you don't feel like it.'

The cliff path took me to the sands at Scott's Bay. Up on the bluff was the lovely house that Richard Burton and Elizabeth Taylor once considered as a Welsh dacha. There's a door in the wall on the edge of the garden. I opened it and descended the steps into a stone alcove which shelters St Anthony's Well. St Anthony, the first Christian hermit, had a strong influence on the early Celtic church; and tradition holds that the Welsh hermit Antwn, who had taken the saint's name, lived around here in the sixth century. It's a gem, this little niche, suggesting the peace and simplicity of a hermit's cell.

The path wound round from the Tywi to the Taf. On the spit of land that reaches into the estuary I came to the farm called Pilgrim's Rest, so called because it was a stopping place on the road to St David's. Pilgrims were good business in medieval times. They needed food, lodging and entertainment and formed the basis of the tourist business of the day. An old building at the farm has three supporting arches, similar to those depicted on the Bayeux Tapestry. The cellar rooms date from the twelfth century.

Llanfihangel Abercywyn: pilgrims' way

Crossing the stream, I came to the ruins of Llanfihangel Abercywyn church, and, under the untamed yews, among the brambles and nettles, found six graves, possibly those of pilgrims. The stones are intriguing, decorated with primitive carvings: men on horseback, the image of a child. It is a half-hidden, little-visited place, a wonder of Wales. I found it haunting.

Not far from here there is another curiosity. It's a tall hedge, about three centuries old. It does not wander like a drunk, as hedges often do, but marches like a minister, in a straight line, for

two and a half miles. Farther on, other medieval hedges cross it, at
right angles. One explanation is that they were a logical way of
ordering a large estate.

Unlikely as it sounds, there is a link between the farm house at
Trefenty ... and the moon. This was where, early in the seventeenth century, Sir William Lower developed his telescope with
lenses made by his friend John Protheroe; and with it he made the
observations that enabled him to draw what was, perhaps, the first
map of the moon.

I had wondered how I would cross the Taf to Laugharne. A
boat was a possibility, but then Jeff Davies, a farmer whose land
runs to the water, offered to walk me across at low tide. This is not
something you should attempt without expert guidance. The route
across changes frequently and you need local knowledge. Jeff told
me stories about people trapped and nearly drowned by the treacherous waters; and he himself had a narrow escape when, engrossed
in fishing, he was struck by the tidal bore.

We had quite a walk, the water rushing and tugging at our feet.
'Keep going,' Jeff said. 'If you stop you get into trouble.' I kept
going.

Soon I was on narrow Cliff Walk above the most famous building in Laugharne, the Boat House, where Dylan Thomas lived for

Write place: the Boat House, Laugharne

Imaginer's chair

the last four years of his life. He said he loved Laugharne 'beyond all places in Wales', though he was troubled by gout and the Inland Revenue. I peeped through the window into the nearby shed, the anvil of his words, where he contemplated the estuary and wrote most of *Under Milk Wood*. Crumpled balls of paper lay on the floor and I wondered about the scribble they contained, the rejected lines and scratched-out thoughts declared unfit for active service.

I had a delightful talk with Jane Dark, who has lived most of her life in Laugharne and knew Dylan well. She led me through her scrapbook – I thought of it as The Great Book of Laugharne – full of photographs, news cuttings and her own commentaries. She proudly showed me, too, the *Under Milk Wood* mural she painted. It fills a wall of her bedroom.

As it happened, she cut Dylan's hair before he set off on the trip to America which ended with his death in 1953.

'Lovely,' he told her, when she had finished snipping. 'It'll last me a lifetime.'

I visited his grave, with its stark white cross standing out clearly among all the other memorials on the hillside above the street of Georgian houses.

I was lucky enough to be in Laugharne on a day that the Corporation met in the Town Hall. With its Grand Jury, Portreeve,

Common Attorneys, Bailiff, Chaplain, Aldermen, Burgesses, Recorders and Grand Jury, the Corporation solemnly celebrates the charter granted by Edward I in the thirteenth century. It sounds like a convocation of Toby jugs, but nothing better demonstrates the sheer mystery and power of tradition.

The Corporation owns seventy-six plots of land, awarded to Burgesses and held until they die. The Portreeve wears a chain of gold cockleshells. On his election night he visits every pub in town and stands everyone a drink; and he also pays for a civic breakfast. Still, there is never a shortage of candidates for the job.

Coygen Hill: double your money

The path from Laugharne took me towards Coygen Hill, partly eaten away by a quarry. In Roman times the hill was the hideout of forgers. Out here, a safe distance from the nearest imperial authorities, they melted down Roman coins and made two out of each one. You can see some of their work in the National Museum in Cardiff.

It was not easy to find the footpath in places. It was overgrown by thick jungles of brambles. But I finally made it over the last furlongs into the pretty village of Llanddowror, a good place to end an absorbing walk. The village hero is the Reverend Griffith Jones, a shepherd boy who became a preacher and who lived in Llanddowror for forty-five years. He is widely regarded as the greatest Welshman of the eighteenth century. He was an educator whose outstanding achievement was to start the popular 'circulating schools' which spread literacy in the countryside. More than three thousand of them were established. They would be set up in a place for three months and then move on, teaching children and adults to read the Welsh bible and the Anglican catechism.

I made my way back to Llansteffan to keep a date with a Tywi fish, freshly caught and cooked by Bill Hill.

Tywi Estuary, Llansteffan: fish and trips